JOURNEYS
WITHIN THE SOUL

*A Former Foster Child's Story of
Trauma to Triumph*

DIANNE R. JACKSON

TABLE OF CONTENTS

DEDICATION AND ACKNOWLEDGMENTS

Of course, there is only one person on earth I want to dedicate my book to, the person who played the most significant role in these chapters. Ms. King, thank you for being constant and always encouraging me! My life is enhanced by your presence, and I love you with everything in me. You have exceeded my expectations and continue to amaze me with your unconditional love.

Ms. King needs a book dedicated to the amazing individual she is. She single-handedly stood by my side from the day I met her until now. She decided from the time I entered high school until today, to stay in my life and assume the role of a mom. I am blessed by her presence and honestly amazed that she cherishes me as much as she does. I have never had to question her love. She can do no wrong in my eyes! I may wish that she played a stronger role in certain aspects of my life, but she sincerely does the best that she knows how and has asked me countless times how she can be more of what I need.

Unfortunately, I do not have the answer to that. I think that is one of the negative sides of growing up in a system that opens your eyes to the reality that the world is not a naturally loving place. People generally love their children and their families but love outside of that is not a given. I have come to accept this, and I love very hard on the people who have chosen to love me. She not only checks up on me but she encourages me, defends me, advocates for me, chastises me and even prays for me! There was a long time when I created a pity party because I never had a relationship with my maternal or paternal grandparents, any aunts or uncles or even my parents. But I have what I have, and I am grateful for that. I know that she was sent to be a part of my life, and I thank God for her every time I think about it. I wish our relationship was more reciprocal but she taught me that all relationships don't work like that and that's OK. She said she is supposed to be there for me, to be a support, a guide, etc., and if she feels that our roles should reverse or be "equal", she'll let me know.

To come to grips with the understanding that someone wants to be there for you with no strings attached takes a lot of learning and unlearning but more than anything, I hope she knows that I appreciate her and she never has to question that!

All honor to God, who dealt with me doubting him and crying out in the darkness asking, "Why me? ... Don't you love me?" as he worked behind the scenes to bless and elevate me when people tried their hardest to destroy the light within. I can't promise that my faith is perfect but we are locked in for life, and I trust you with my life! You were there, and I hope everyone gets to experience the love you have for them.

I would like to acknowledge and thank all of the people who made this book possible! I reached out to many of you to let you know that I'd mention you in my book, and every single one of you was supportive and excited and never asked me to leave any of our precious moments out!

Dedication and Acknowledgments

To Ms. King- Thanks for writing my forward and being willing to learn me and love me the way that I asked to be. That means the world to me, as do you! You had every right to move on with your life after I graduated as you had already gone above and beyond, but you decided that I was worth a lifetime commitment, and I am extremely thankful.

To Mrs. Evans- I hope I honored our story! You were so instrumental to who I am and I am eternally grateful to you and your family and what you've done for me. Thank you!

To Juanita & Family- Our story wasn't always pretty, but we're past that now! I hope you honor my truth and my perspective.

To Z- Who would've known that me reaching out to you about this book and your role in it would help us realize that God writes the best love stories? Though our story is toward the end of this book, I am so excited about all of our new beginnings!

To the reader: Many of the names have been changed. I hope this book evokes change in you! May you orient your heart closer to God and to the one of most defenseless populations, the children who are parent-deficient. The saying that there are two sides to every story and then there's the truth makes so much sense as I get older.In my younger days I would say that my side was the truth but boy perception will leave you really seeing things not as they were but from your own reality which is shaped in your past, your insecurities and whatever else your mind wants you to see. Here's my truth and my story.

FOREWORD

A rose is still a rose, and no matter where the seed starts, it will still become a rose. In this case, the rose is Ms. Dianne Jackson. She epitomizes what a strong, sophisticated, loving woman is. The trials and tribulations she has gone through in her short time on earth have made her into a woman not to be taken advantage of. Knowing her, I am confident that from birth, God knew who she would become, had a role for her to play, and protected her every step of the way. He always brought her through and still does. She is a living testimony that cannot be ignored once you read her story.

I met Dianne during her freshman year in high school and from the outside, she was a typical teen that took part in activities that teens tend to involve themselves in. Sometimes being a little mischievous as teens are, but she always kept a smile on the face of the adults in the school, including mine. Once you got to know her story and the pain she has endured, you knew that she was atypical. She survived storms most adults could not but every day, she kept a smile on her face and earned stellar grades in high school, which earned her admittance into Marquette University. What kept her so strong at that young age I've often asked myself, but the answer is clear: She was protected even when she did not know the magnificent power of God's protection. It is no surprise now that I met her. I believe God ordained our paths to cross for His work and His will. I never envisioned that at my juncture in life, she would become family. As a school counselor, I knew I had to be there for the children I served, but I never thought those connections would last more than 20 years.

Like most educators, we want to serve our children and get them ready for the life they will encounter all the while showing them love and empathy as best as we can with the little time we have with them. Dianne showed me that it goes beyond the walls you are surrounded by during your time together, and that the relationship formed can last forever. In my training to become a school counselor, I read all the time about children and the problems they can encounter, but seeing it is a different story. Dianne's story demonstrates that smiles are not always true, that children can be strong with the right support even if they do not have it at home, and that no matter where you begin, it does not dictate how you end. She was not supposed to be where she is today. Statistically, she was supposed to be a negative statistic, but instead, she is a positive statistic. She could have taken the easy way out and used her experience as an excuse to not be productive, to spread negativity, and to do harm to people. Instead, she took the negativity and disappointments she experienced from others and turned it positive. She opens her heart to others even when they do not deserve it. Sometimes it is reciprocated and sometimes it isn't, but she continues to love and to be a beacon of hope for all God brings in her path. She is a dreamcatcher because she provides opportunities for others to pursue their dreams by opening up her home, her pocketbook, her time, and her heart. Sometimes, I fuss at her because she deserves all the love she pours into others. I will admit that she has grown in this area, but her giving of herself is who she is. It is part of her fabric. She couldn't breathe and survive if she wasn't helping someone. Again, God knew her role when she was conceived, and that is why she is with us today.

I hope you are inspired by her story. Every time I talk to her, I'm in awe of her because for Ms. Jackson, life has not been a crystal stair.

INTRODUCTION

This book has been in my heart, mind and soul ever since I was about 12 years old. I remember discussing writing a book in therapy one day, and just like the disconnected therapists they were in those days, they encouraged me to write but thought I meant books of fiction. I am sure they thought they were having a breakthrough by supporting my interest. It left me a bit confused and while I tried to go that path of fiction, that wasn't what my heart desired, so I abandoned that dream ... for a while.

Then, one day in college while sitting in the amazing and insightful Mr. Alexander Pete's office having a personal talk that had nothing to do with writing a book, he began to prophesy. His words went something like, "You're gonna write a book. It is going to change lives. It will turn into a play and become very lucrative for you. So lucrative that you will have homes in different states and so much money that you will begin to give very generously to others."

Yes! I was as shocked and surprised as you all are reading it. Writing this memoir wasn't an unfamiliar thought, but I never considered the impact. While it recharged me, I did not go home and start writing immediately.

Then, just like God does when he wants to make sure you understand the assignment, he confirms it. About two weeks later, I went with a friend to a church service and they had a prophecy line. I wasn't going to join the line because I was used to false prophets and didn't want to hear superfluous language with no real spiritual insight. However, she joined the line and since I was her guest, I was obliged to simply "go through the motions." When I got face to face with the prophet, he told me a very similar thing about this book I would write. By now, I was floored and knew I had to answer the call.

I went home and began to map out my book. Wrote a few lines here, decided the title, and then got busy with life. I got distracted by the grief, the fun, and my newfound freedom of adulthood, and I never completed that book. That was about 15 years ago.

Then, in recent years, that book began to call out to me (not literally. I am a writer, y'all, I don't hear voices) and I knew I needed to finish it. But then I started to worry about how people would feel who were not so nice to me and would be called out in my book, so I pushed the book to the side again.

Yet in the past 2 years, I devoted my life to self-improvement and returning to therapy. During these sessions, my therapist encouraged me to write and publish the book and not worry about what people felt about my truth. It wasn't an immediate sale, but eventually, I got here.

I wrote the book and then life got crazy. Four months after I finished the book, my father died. From there, the year was rocky, with many ups and downs, and the book was again pushed to the side.

But now we're here, and I am so excited to share this book and allow it to do what God wants it to. This is a total leap of faith as I am a very private person who prides myself on having a mystique, but my journey was for so many others to know they, too, can triumph from trauma.

PROLOGUE

Just When

My truth reads like fallacy
How could loss and tragedy end so beautifully?
How could deep lows get high again?
How can I throw up my hands and still win?... How can?
How can I forsake hope and hope shows up again?
...

Nuggets of wisdom to take on your journey

You will need these as you navigate this book. Take a post-it note and come back as you need to ...even as you need them in your own life. One thing that trauma has afforded me is a deep knowing, understanding and realizing. I've done the work so you don't have to.

....

What a beautiful place to be in when you discover the fallibility of who we are as people... because then we can see that it is God who has done all these marvelous things that we get credit for... and then we can praise him because every good and perfect thing comes from him! ... And we can thank him for the love.

...

Some people may not understand your dreams because it's too big for them. Stay focused and be careful who you share what with. It's not always that they are haters... some people can only dream in a box and they've got your limits there too. Show them.

...

I have learned to never be too certain. Leave room to be enlightened and refuted. Never be too stubborn to change because anything that's not growing is dead.

...

Job of the bible once said during his time of suffering: "so you can accept the good from God but not the trouble? " - Job 2:10 ...Let's not do that - he's building and blessing in the midst of the storm!

...

I see so many reasons to complain and so many reasons to give thanks.I'll choose the latter.Life is hard ... let's find joy where we can.

...

I have learned that where people stand in terms of Triumph, Tragedy and Trial shows who they really are for it is very easy to keep face in still waters. In the triad of these three you learn about true friendships and true faith.

...

Prologue

Things wouldn't be so sweet without the bitter

Summer wouldn't feel so great without the winter

So embrace the balance of life ... see God be BIG!

Bask in his ability to be great EVERY TIME!

...

You can never be an overachiever because there is always more to achieve!

RESPECT- ROOT SPECT::: TO SEE... Respect is taking the time to see from someone else's perspective ... not agreeing but seeing...Can I see you if I'm bitter? If I'm holding onto right? If I speak in summation vs. facts? If I tailor the story to emphasize certain points and minimize others?Where is the middle? How can two reach there free of the bondage of bitterness? What happens when one is willing and the other is appealing?

...

Everything isn't an attack. Sometimes it's critical feedback streamlined with facts !

...

If you can do anything right, it is to admit when you're wrong!

...

I am further convinced that I am right where I'm supposed to be !Let us all commit to seeking God for direction and allowing him to lead in all ways .It's working for my good and I want the same for all of you ! Seize the day !

...

Opposition of God vs. opposition of man can appear almost identical.

This is why our relationship with God is important.

Everyone we love, the people we love will disappoint us but that's because we are all broken . Is their hurting you intentional and worthy of dismissal or is this a part of your long suffering?

If I'm transparent, I was evaluating my relationship with someone and everything in me told me to run...retreat etc. and I actually told them that I was done.

I went to God and told Him that I wanted to pray for this individual as I knew they were hurting but they hurt my feelings so I couldn't.

I decided to be transparent and let them know the tug and pull I was feeling and they began to reveal that they were indeed hurt and putting up walls and barriers.

That insight gave me enough to soften my heart and take them to the altar. While in prayer, God reminded me that " love is longsuffering" and it was okay to fight for this person and relationship.

Prologue

That doesn't mean that we will always have a close relationship but at this time, I am on an assignment.

There is a place and level in God where you have to "put your money where your mouth is" and do uncomfortable things that God asks you to do.

If you think I'm lying read the story of Job, Jonah, Moses or Saul...

The beauty is that the Holy Spirit gives us peace and that peace enabled me to separate my personal feelings from this situation.

Lesson: Let's take people to God in prayer, take our hands off and see what God says is next for that situation instead of making those decisions for ourselves with our limited, broken and jaded perspectives.

...

Life is a beautiful surprise. The hardships will come but there is sunshine on the other side of the mountain.

...

Victory for me - has never been a straight line...However there is so much abundance on the other side.

...

And we know that in all things God works for the good of those who love him, who have been called according to his purpose.- Romans 8:28 Therefore know that God is working things out and everything isn't how it appears!

...

God always has a " ram in the bush" ... If He said he'll do it, He will! Don't let your current circumstances distract you from how big our God is and how His promises NEVER RETURN VOID!

...

To settle in any form of your life whether it be relationships, career etc. says "I'm not worthy"... and I know that I am more valuable than any second rate anything, that's why I won't settle. I realize for many that the false realities of broken relationships and failed ambitions paint a picture of what some see as law. I on the other hand know that my Father has all control and if he loves and accepts me being that he is perfect...I can't even fathom expecting less out of this life *waiting*

...

Don't ever neglect yourself! Self care is paramount on your journey.

"When Nature Calls"

Admittedly, sometimes I ignore phone calls not because I'm busy
But because I'm not
I'm enjoying the whispers of nature
How the tiny dew drops show me purpose
The wind once told me that we are multi-faceted
There is a time to be gentle
And there is a time to be tumultuous
But if you destroy, you must build

Prologue

And destruction is only for construction
Because the only other option is vanity
And vanity ...is merely chasing the wind
-5/29/2015

...

Throughout my entire life I continue to see just how "big"
God is . Like seriously... There have been times I attempted
to cry because of how it looked but in my subconscious ,
I knew my Father would fix it and there was no reason to
fret. I encourage anyone who feels instability to hold tight
and pray . Through obedience and humility he will ride
you through this ocean we call life . God is truly amazing .

...

Ch.1

ROAD TO FOSTER CARE

efore foster care and the divide of my family, there was a man and a woman on a journey of their own. I think that I have learned to separate my parents from their mistakes and have learned to look at them as individuals.

From what I know, my parents met in Chicago and had my older siblings there. They relocated to Milwaukee before I was born. It is said that my mother was following my father, who was following his mother (my grandmother, who died before I was born).

What I can infer is that two very young individuals decided to love each other and build a family ill-equipped. Ill-equipped, because without the proper definition of love and no intentional family planning but intentional acts of sexual intimacy is the origin of my story.

My father was tall, slim and dark-skinned. He always had a mustache and a beard. He liked rocking a hoop earring in one ear and was a lover of Tupac, poetry and old country-western movies. He was always on the go, and loved to dress up (either in suits or Jordans) and to dance. I don't remember my mother without drawn-on eyebrows. She's brown-skinned, of average height and heavyset. She is a lover of get-togethers and celebrations. She's also a lover of old-school music and dominos.

My parents made all of us kids in the 70s and 80s. This was the time when crack ran rampant in the ghettos and my parents would partake and succumb to the power of this drug. No one knew the effects back then. All most people knew was that it gave them a high and an escape from their harsh realities. I have learned to absolve my parents of any guilt and humanize them again. Yes, they are my parents but they are more than just that. They were two individuals seeking healing while trying to raise eight children.

My mother was 13 when she got pregnant for the first time. I am not sure when she started having sex, but I know at some point it wasn't by choice. My mother was an only child and she once detailed how her mother allowed men to rape her to pay bills. I am not sure about my father's upbringing besides the fact that he had siblings whom he loved dearly.

I believe my parents loved each other. There were times where they were very much into each other, laughing and giddy. Now that I am an adult, I realize that my parents came from broken families that didn't prepare them for relationships of any kind let alone one that involved kids. If you mix that with an addiction to drugs, it can only evolve into something destructive and when my parents were high and drunk, destructive wasn't even a strong enough word.

My memories include my father clumsily bumping into things after being drunk and them having very violent fights. What I learned from my paperwork was something that remained a mystery for a long time. I never understood why my father spent so much time in jail. I learned that he was physically abusive to my mother. While they both would be exchanging blows he would hit my mother so hard that he broke bones and there were times when she struggled to walk and function based on the intensity of the fights. There were definitely knives used, people stabbed and things thrown. Years later, I saw some of my siblings take this approach in their relationships with their significant others.

I'd like to think that my memory is astute and what I do remember, I recall in massive detail but I remember very little about their fights. I'd imagine my mind compressed those memories because God deemed them too heavy to carry. It breaks my heart to think of my siblings as little babies having to witness such violence and being so afraid and only having each other for support. Many people have lots to say about the state of protective services, and I have my own issues because the state did a terrible job of protecting my siblings and I, but we also did not need to continue to live like we were living before their intervention.

Also contrary to popular belief, the state did its due diligence to not remove us from the home initially. They offered my mother support by way of daycare for us younger kids, food stamps, etc. But my mother's task was difficult. She had eight kids with very little family support. She was an only child, and her relationship with her mother was fragmented.

Now that I am an adult, I can place everything in perspective. Then, I wasn't able to. I felt insulted that my mother wanted to share how her mother didn't protect her, as I held back all the things in the system that happened to me. Now, I am grateful that she shared that with me. It helped me to cry for the little girl and young woman she was as I read my history on paper just a few years back. When I think of my mother now, I hope she knows that there is no ill will. I want more than anything for her to be free from guilt and shame. I cannot imagine feeling guilty most of her life. There has to be some guilt that comes with performing sex acts for money even if you don't want to, and guilt for not being able to raise your children. Each time I pray for my mother, I pray for the freedom of her mind! God doesn't want us to carry shame or guilt! I'd always pray that her and my father were free in their minds because I love them both and prayed incessantly for their healing. They deserve to be happy!

My father's violence towards my mother certainly doesn't match how affectionate he was. He was always an affectionate man. Until his passing, he'd still call all his kids pet names. He used to terrify me by tossing me in the air as a form of being playful, but he loved to do fatherly things like that. He always made sure to hug us and always said he loved us. My mother was good about saying she loved us, too. Unlike most fathers, mine was not afraid to cry. I saw my father cry when we were taken, and every time our visits came to a close. He also wrote poetry and thought on an intellectual level. There is so much of me that I see in my father, not to mention everyone used to say I look like him.

For all the readers of this book whose stories connect to mine, one of the greatest lessons I've learned in terms of forgiveness and healing is to see people as three-dimensional. They are not only people who hurt us but people who are broken at the core of themselves. This is how God can love us so sincerely! He sees the challenges we face and our fragmented senses of reality. We're all just broken people on a quest to healing on a *journey within our soul.*

I also wanted to include these things because as I explore the trauma I faced, I want my readers to understand the dimensions of my very broken parents who did all they could with the pieces they had.

Living with my parents was chaotic for sure. I was shot in the head with a BB gun and had a glass bottle thrown at me in the heat of an argument between my parents. I have heard both stories, and I only remember the aftermath. I know I had to have plastic surgery to repair the skin that was hanging off as a result. From what my parents told me (the BB gun story), my brothers used to bully kids in the neighborhood, and I was the revenge. They waited for the opportunity to pay them back and they chose me. I had visions of that day for a long time. I do remember an extreme amount of blood pouring down my face and into my eyes, but I remember the paramedics and I remember going into shock. I thank God that it hit me perfectly in the center of my head, and I did not lose an eye. I am also grateful that the skin continues to brown at the same speed at the skin around it. I actually forget that my scar exists until some curious person points to their head and says, "What happened right here?"

We were extremely hungry at times. I'll never forget the day we all got a piece of bread and mine dropped in the toilet. I tried to fish it out until I realized I didn't like slimy bread. Then there was the time my older brother LJ/Moog (Lloyd) and I sat in a pantry with a box of spaghetti.

As we ate the uncooked noodles, we told each other what we were really eating. We'd said things like, "I'm eating chips, whatchu eating?" and for a moment, we enjoyed our delicious meal choices with full bellies.

There was also the time I tried to drink a 40 one of the house guests had left outside their door. I had to be a very small child as I was not much bigger than the drink itself and I did not have the strength to turn it over to drink from, but I sure did try! I can still see this image in my head! We were left to our own devices often and not supervised as we should've been.

My older brothers also took pride in torturing me, or had me doing ridiculous things so they could laugh. I was very aware of their antics but sometimes I played along anyhow. My mother had one daughter, followed by four boys, and I came along 10 years after having her one and only girl. So there was a bit of excitement about my arrival. However, my brothers were mischievous! They'd drop my sister, younger brother, and I off at daycare and then play in the windows. When the daycare workers looked out the window, they'd be nowhere to be found. Once they did catch them, they were so furious! That game went on so long where they continued to find what we were laughing at in the window that when they finally caught my brothers, they got in so much trouble! Reflecting on that incident helps me realize just how harsh we are on our black boys. What they did was silly, but you would've thought they killed a cat the way the daycare providers reacted. They were yelled at, chastised, and warned as if they were adults. At this time, my older brothers were between the ages of 5 and 11.

Once one of my older brothers gave me Monopoly money and told me to purchase a few items from the corner store. I was 3 or 4 and I definitely knew the difference between real and fake money, but I decided to humor him. I went right into the store while he watched from a distance and tried to make the purchases he requested. After I put the money on the counter and turned to leave, I was stopped. My brother got a good laugh and I couldn't care less even though I think a part of him was hoping I got away before I was caught.

Some of the antics my brothers played weren't so light-hearted.The craziest thing they ever did was hold me over a bridge as the cars drove past below. My mother was furious! She lined each of them up against a wall and whipped the mischief out of them that day.

It is important to mention (even though this is a given) especially with this being the first chapter that this is from my perspective. Speaking to my brother LJ (Lasko) who is 5 years older than me helped put things in perspective. Our place in the family is interesting. He is the third from the top and I am the third from the bottom. Our views weren't different but he experienced and understood the drama at a deeper level being older and male.

For as long as I can remember, I had a memory of being at my grandmother's house when I was really young. All of my life I thought that memory took place in Chicago because I knew she lived there before she passed and for as long as I can remember. Yet he told me that we actually lived with my grandmother for a short time when I was the baby. He said that that was the only time he remembered being a child entirely. He even spoke about knowing our mother before the drugs. He talked about how she worked hard to provide for us, and that my father not only introduced my mother to drugs but would also take the money to provide for his habit.

Lasko told me how he assumed the role of the oldest because he was the third from the top and my eldest sister and brother were not home much. To put this into perspective. My older siblings were 12 and 14 when we were taken by the state, and Lasko was 9. He described how he spent many nights babysitting us. He was my mother's protector. When my dad fought her "like a man" (in my brother's words), he would do his best to call the cops. He noted how each time he got caught, even when he ran to use the payphone.

He provided me with a story when he detailed his spirit being broken. He said my mother always told him that he did not have to call the cops, but he felt very passionate about doing so ... he wanted so desperately to be my mother's hero. The most traumatic time was when my father had beat my mother again, this time for the rent money. My mother had started giving the rent money to Lasko so that if he looked for it, he couldn't find it. Some kind of way he got wind that my brother had it, but my brother was already at the payphone and started telling the dispatcher that he needed a police officer. Right before he could give the address, my father had caught up to him and started beating him. Lasko said that he wasn't even disappointed that he was beaten; he was disappointed that he couldn't save my mother or himself that day, and he desperately wanted to successfully save her.

He told me that there were so many times when he cried in agony for help. No one helped him. They just watched and didn't intervene. He also gave me insight to a mother

I never knew. A mother before drugs who he was proud of ... who did her best to make a home and provide for her children.

We were taken into the foster system on Sept. 5, 1990, one of my older brothers' birthdays (Clintone's). The day started like any other, except there was a knock at the door. It was not until I read my history on paper a few years back that I understood that there was much interference from CPS trying to work with my mother (and father when he wasn't incarcerated) and help her/them keep us. Looking at the full picture as described in the paperwork, I had to grieve with and for my mother. My mother had eight children in 12 years.By the time she was 26, we were all conceived. She was living in Milwaukee with few family members to reach and her and my father's relationship was rocky . He wasn't absent when he wasn't in jail, but it was a toxic relationship.

The day we were taken is one that plays like a movie in my mind .The day felt very random but as I have recently read in the reports, the day was not random at all. Everyone has their negative things to say about the system but from my experience, they really do try to keep families together.

When they came, they came like a raid. The police had a paddy wagon waiting for us, and we didn't have time to pack anything. Half of us couldn't find shoes and we left only in T-shirts. Everybody was so emotional, but I was like a fly on the wall. I just watched everyone's reactions and though I was at peace, I cried because it seemed like that was the thing to do. This was the beginning of my journey within the system, and my strong sense of God's voice and direction.

As I reflect back on the younger years of my life, I never understood why I could be at ease in very traumatic situations. To be clear, the trauma *did* affect me! But at the moment, I was non-reactive. For as long as I can remember, that was my countenance. It is amazing to see how much God was building me up for all times I'd need that skill later in life. I'd need to self-regulate and self-soothe so many times on my journey, so I am grateful, even though I didn't understand back then.

2 Timothy 3:14-17 NIV 14 But as for you, continue in what you have learned and have become convinced of, because you know those from whom you learned it, 15 and how from infancy you have known the Holy Scriptures, which are able to make you wise for salvation through faith in Christ Jesus. 16 All Scripture is God-breathed and is useful for teaching, rebuking, correcting and training in righteousness, 17 so that the servant of God may be thoroughly equipped for every good work.

While this scripture may appear displaced to you, bear with me and watch it come alive as I tell my story. My goal is to turn an atheist into a believer and a believer into someone with unwavering faith even during their darkest times. That's what my journey has done to me and even with all of the trials, I am blessed.

Ch.2

TO THE TORTURE CHAMBER

Before we were divided and placed in separate foster homes, we lived in a facility that felt like heaven to me. We lived in a building with several other kids to play with! I remember being able to ask that the skin be cut off my apple and when I wet the bed, they simply changed the sheets. That facility was a stark contrast to the foster homes I'd soon be placed in.

One of my earliest memories in a foster home was the Smiths. The Smiths were a woman and her teenage daughter. Ms. Smith was a light-skinned middle-aged woman who was slightly heavyset. Her cheeks had several moles on both sides. Her daughter was slender and dark-skinned with long hair. We were merely a paycheck to Ms. Smith, and it was very clear based on how my younger sister (Terricka) and I were treated.

I wish I could remember times of joy or intentional love shown to my sister and I but I can definitively say that the only love and joy that was shown was the love and joy my sister and I created with each other.

There was this one time my sister and I were playing outside. I was no more than 5 years old which means my sister was only 2 or 3 years old. We were playing on the side of the house inside the gate when we became hungry. With my sister being so young and us living in a strange place, she took her cues from me.

I told her that we should go in and tell them that we were hungry. We did and the lady (Ms. Smith) told us to go play and she would make something shortly. Some time went on and we noticed that they hadn't called us in to eat so we decided to protest (my idea). Because I was the oldest and my sister listened to whatever I said, we marched up and down the side of the house saying, "We want some food... we want some food!" We did this for a while until we were called into the house.

When we entered the house, we saw a loaf of bread worth of sandwiches on the table. At first my sister and I were extremely excited at the large platter but after about a sandwich and a half, we were full and ready to depart. We were informed that since we were impatient and couldn't wait to be fed we would have to eat every single one. We ate as many as we could until we started to throw them back up. She had no mercy and that is the only thing that saved us from finishing those sandwiches.

This house was truly torture. She never physically disciplined us with objects to our body, she disciplined us in worse ways...ways that would damage our spirit, threaten our safety and affect us emotionally for years to come.

This food torture was not a one time event! I can still see this image in my mind. Here we were with nice Easter dresses on and sitting in front of the TV. Ms. Smith had a friend that took a liking to us and brought us a solid chocolate Easter bunny of our own. Solid as in it wasn't hollow on the inside. It was very thick chocolate. The bunny seemed very large in my memory. Perhaps it was 6 inches or maybe even a foot. What I do know for sure is it *was not* a small piece of chocolate candy. We were so excited about our candy that we begged and begged for it. To be honest, we were young so I am not sure how many times we asked and how frequently she had to endure our constant begging for the treat. When she got tired of us asking, she gave us our chocolate bunnies. What started off as joy and excitement quickly turned to a painful memory. She made us eat it until we threw it up! That day and at least the next my sister and I took turns sitting in front of the television and regurgitating in the toilet.

To make matters worse, I had a bad bedwetting issue. At this time I was only 5, but I would continue to wet myself in my sleep until I was about 12. I tried my hardest to get up at night, but I had several dreams that I was up in the bathroom when I was actually in the bed.

Ms. Smith tried several things to prevent bedwetting. She limited my water intake close to bed time. She placed a plastic sheet under the sheets and had me wear pullups to bed but nothing worked. Each day's consequence was the same: a discipline tactic that would put me within inches of my life.

She would fill the bathtub with cold water, tie my legs and feet together with long adult-size socks and submerge my entire body in water being sure to push my head down anytime I would try to come to the surface for air. Each day, I would fight to survive this torture and when she felt satisfied, she would take me out of the water. This was so traumatic for me. That level of violence and sincere fear for my life was the scariest thing I endured to that point. I cannot understand how someone looks at an innocent child and holds their head down in water to the point that they could die, and continues life as normal. Her teenage daughter was a co-conspirator. If she struggled to complete this viciously violent task alone, her daughter was surely there to support her.

By this time I could separate my mind, body, and spirit. My mind would conjure an escape, my body would fight with all my might to be free, but my spirit would be watching. I vividly remember being outside my body having this experience, feeling helpless and in agony. Since I couldn't stop myself from wetting the bed, I had to come up with a different plan.

One time we had a visit with our mother and she was getting ready to give me my "pee punishment." I told her that if she agreed not to drown me that day, I wouldn't go with my mother and she agreed. I remember when my mom came to the door to pick us up and she told her that I didn't want to come. I will never forget the look of disappointment on my mother's face! I wanted to tell her the truth, and I definitely wanted to go with her. I was so hurt but more so terrified. I felt that since no one could protect me, I had to keep this house of torture to myself.

I feel bad about this, but I would be dishonest if I did not say it. I once lied and said my sister "peed on me" in order to escape the torture. It didn't work and she pretended not to know who to discipline so she decided to place us both in the water and therefore my sister had to suffer because of me.

In addition to that incident, my sister was born with a genetic disorder called syndactyly. It means that her fingers were born fused together. When she entered the system, they decided that she needed surgery to get them separated. One day she came home with medicine and separated fingers. Our foster mother was not good about giving my sister her medicine regularly, and there were times she would cry out in pain. When my sister (no older than 3) would cry out in this way, our foster mother would give her the medicine and make her stand in the corner until it kicked in and she stopped crying. It was in these moments that I first learned to separate myself from the deep love I had for my sister. I wanted to comfort her, but I wasn't allowed, and I rarely cried as I knew there was no comfort if I did. So I blocked out her screams and told myself it didn't matter. This would inform our relationship for years to come, and I hate that it broke me in that way.

I am not sure why we left that house as they just don't express those things when you are young, but I know God had something to do with it. It is my hope that they get everything that they have coming to them. I don't understand how you can intentionally hurt a child and not feel any sadness whatsoever, and while I am a proponent of mercy and have the ability to want compassion, I am not ashamed to say that I want(ed) God's wrath on her life.

Although I am healed from the trauma, I also am OK with wanting them to receive their full karma. There are a lot of times when I have asked God to show compassion and his mercy but this was not one of them. I don't dwell on those events, and I rarely think about this family at all, but memories have a way of creeping in even as we're on our healing journey.

For example, if I turn on the shower and expect warm water but it's unexpectedly cold, a flashback of being held down in that arctic water will resurface in my mind. I have learned to be present in these times, being able to be grateful for my present but fully aware and acknowledging the past. It also reminds me that I still have soul work to do, and I have to be aware that good and bad, my past has shaped me.

Ch.3

Shift to Silvia's

It has been more than 25 years since I have lived at Silvia's house, but I remember everything! I remember how the house was laid out. I remember all of their names. I remember how they treated me. I remember how they all had Jheri curls minus the youngest child...how most of the backyard was rocks and not grass...even how there was a large circular table in the dining room where we ate.

Silvia was a dark-skinned woman of medium build who had gold teeth. She was in her late 30s to mid 40s. AJ was around the same age, and dark-skinned as well. He had a mustache and facial hair. AJ Jr.'s appearance is a blur to me, but I remember Shaletha had a Jheri curl, that was about neck length. She was of medium build and had brown gums. She was between 18 and 25. Tierra had a medium complexion, was thin and wore her hair in either braids or ponytails. She looked very different from the other siblings.

Silvia had three children: two daughters and one son. Shaletha and AJ Jr. were teens while Tierra was somewhere around our age. Silvia was married to a man named AJ. This was the early 90s so Silvia, Shaletha and AJ all rocked a Jheri curl. There was only one nice person in that house. That was Silvia's husband, but he only extended kindness when she wasn't around. When she was present, she extended all discipline and consequences to us, and he was never present in those moments.

The sexual abuse started early. Every timeSilvia ran an errand, my sister and I were abused by Shaletha. Her sexual abuse was gruesome and strange. She locked her sister away. AJ Jr. was always occupied upstairs or gone, and she had us perform sexual acts on her. She would press our mouths up against her vagina and say "Lick it." She inserted sticks inside herself and made us suck on the other end, or directly on her vagina. She'd even made us suck on her breasts. My sister and I were terrified, and we looked each other in the eye hoping that the other one had a plan, but we didn't, so we tearfully followed every command. She threatened to beat us if we ever told, and that was also terrifying. We never told Silvia (not that it would have mattered...it might have been to our detriment, to be honest) or anyone else as long as we lived there.

My parents had never laid a hand on us, so to be threatened with physical assault was enough to detour either of us from saying anything. I remember a few times they had whooped my brothers, but I don't remember one time being hit by either of my parents. That all came in foster care.

I was terrified of being beaten. I guess that's why I never told. I think I also didn't feel protected by anyone, so I kept my mouth shut until years later when I no longer lived there.

Silvia also loved to violently discipline us. She had a thick stick that she taped with white tape so that when she whooped us, the stick wouldn't break. This was the same stick that Shaletha stuck in her vagina.

When Silvia noticed that the stick was leaving marks, she adopted a different plan. She hung us upside down and spun us around by our ankles. I remember trying to grab the couch, the phone cord, anything. My terror brought her so much satisfaction. There was no remorse or emotion attached to her actions besides sheer hatred. When she was done, we knew to go to the room and self-soothe until the next time. I think to this day that might be why I'm afraid of rollercoasters. That drop feels like death to me, and I know it's not normal. While everyone can enjoy rides that twist and turn upside down, it gives me major anxiety, and each time I feel like I am going to die of a heart attack.

In addition to that, I partook in some strange experiences that to this day I cannot make sense of. I can only fathom that Silvia was paid for me to be experimented on. The memory is so strange that I'd like to think it was a dream, but I have lived long enough and have had enough spiritual connection to know that what I remember happened.

There was this one time when Silvia and I went to a building. It was just us in a waiting room. She eventually went into a room with someone and left me in the waiting room. The waiting room had a big play treehouse, so I used it to occupy my time. I wasn't nervous to be left alone because so many people made decisions about my life and never had conversations with me, I simply learned to just go with the flow. I was also enjoying this amazing toy. After a while, I needed to relieve myself. I waited a bit for

Silvia to return to take me to the restroom. When I grew tired of waiting, I went to search for the restroom. All the rooms that led out were locked, so I ended up using the bathroom on myself.

Not too long after, Silvia returned to take me into the appointment and discovered that I had used the restroom on myself. She was so upset and it turned out, the restroom was directly in front of me! I could read, but I did not see it! It was above eye level as I was only about 5 or 6 at the time.

Silvia asked for some wipes, took me in the restroom and cleaned me up. She apologized to the "doctor" that I would have no bottoms on for the exam. He told her that it would not be a problem, and that I did not need them. He weighed me and put me on an exam table naked. He then washed his hands and inserted a tube up my vagina and asked me to pee it out. I told him that I did not have to pee because I had just wet myself. Several people entered the room all smiling at me with clipboards in their hands. He went to the sink and proceeded to pour water on my vagina until I peed the tube out. They took some notes and left. I visited this facility a few times and had the same interaction happen. I'll never forget how I came home, dressed and was in my room watching television in childhood bliss when Silvia grabbed that stick and beat me for using the bathroom on myself.

Our first Christmas season was so exciting. Shaletha gave us the rundown. She told us how it must be morning before we came downstairs, and that she'd wake us up. Then we were to wait by the tree until her parents woke up. Once the parents awoke, we'd be handed an abundance of gifts. There we sat in our pj's under the lights of the tree filled with wonderment. Imagine our surprise when Silvia said, "I don't know why y'all excited, y'all not getting nothing but what the social worker sent." So my little sister and I sat and cried and watched them open their gifts. We also watched her pick through what the social worker sent and give all the nice things to Tierra. I think all we were left with was a bear. No one flinched or felt bad for us. Everyone was happy except the invisible children known as my sister and I.

That wasn't the only time we endured that type of intentional hatred. One summer, one of the neighbors came with a bag of hand-me-down clothes that could fit my sister, myself, and Tierra. We were so excited to see who could fit what. As Silvia opened the bag, I grabbed a pink outfit. She abruptly interrupted and said "Nah, you too hot for hot pink," and instructed Tierra to try it on. The joy of what was in the bag was gone, and I simply waited for whatever would be given to me.

One day, my sister got really sick. To remedy her illness, Silvia chopped up some potatoes and made anklets for my sister to wear from them. She laid around in the room all day. At some point, Shaletha went into the room to "check on my sister", and when she brought her out of the room, my sister could not walk or talk. She was speaking in an unknown tongue! My sister was having a seizure! She was taken by ambulance to the hospital that night. To this day, I think my sister was sick and Shaletha went back there and was molesting her, which exacerbated her sickness. That night we did something we did not normally do, we had a huge platter of take-out food and junk food; it was strange! It was as if there was a celebration feast that my sister was sick. Silvia would go visit my sister while she was there but she never took me! The mission to divide was working.

When my sister came home, I was so excited to see her. I asked her how her experience was and she said, " Fun, I got to dance with the doctors." My sister had many seizures in Silvia's house and once we left, they never returned. I know God was working to get us out of there. There is no other explanation for it.

On top of my sister's strange illness, Silvia began to be hospitalized a lot. AJ, her husband who played in the background and was hardly engaged with us, began to be the main parent. He spent his nights with her and part of the day with us. When he wasn't there, we were left with child molester Shaletha, and she definitely took advantage of these times. This is when we saw a nicer side of that house. AJ ordered takeout and generally treated us kindly. As time went on, Silvia's heart condition worsened. But when she wasn't sick, she was no nicer. Silvia had a Ph.D. in crushing a child's spirit. There was not an ounce of love and compassion there.

I believe that my sister suffered the worst abuse. AJ Jr. loved to be upstairs. He had the entire floor to himself, and he and his best friend made it their retreat. One time, he called my sister upstairs and she stayed for a long time. When she returned, I asked her what she was doing and she said, " AJ asked me to suck his thing for a dollar." I asked her if she did it, and she told me no, but I knew my babysitter was not upstairs that long with two teenage/early 20s boys doing nothing! I cannot imagine the horror my sister endured, and to come downstairs as if nothing happened. To this day as I try to ask my sister about these events, she remembers nothing! I believe she suffers from childhood amnesia which is a condition that happens to some people in order to survive childhood.

I am not sure how long we stayed there, but one day we had to leave because Silvia's heart condition was out of control, but I know that was all God!

Ch.4

ꞴRAILS OF ꞴRADITION AND ꞴRAVAIL

$\mathcal{M}$oving to Maria's house was scary:all the moves were. By this time, I learned that image and reality were two different things. I knew that seemingly nice people could be demons in reality. I was cautious and pensive, and I was all of 7.

Maria was a short, thin, light-skinned woman with long, relaxed hair that she kept done in what is known as a wrap (a hairstyle where you wrap your hair around your head at night and once combed down, it has a bounce made by the wrapping procedure). While she loved to keep her hair done, in other aspects of her appearance, she kept it simple. She wore glasses, a big, black purse and mostly jeans and a T-shirt or jeans and a simple shirt of some sort.

Maria's house was stable and predictable. Her youngest daughter was born with some health complications, so she stayed home to take care of her. That meant that most days she was home when we arrived home, and she had made or was making dinner. We were taught basic manners and ways to show respect. You greet everyone when you enter a room. You make eye contact when you speak to someone. If adults are having a conversation, you leave the room and go a far enough distance to not eavesdrop, and if you happen to eavesdrop, you better pretend as if you hadn't.

Maria was old-school. For context it's helpful to note that her parents were sharecroppers. Her mom died when she was young and she was the youngest of all of her siblings and there were many of them (I cannot remember the exact number). So some of her ways of being were also old-school. For example, if you defended yourself by explaining why you did or didn't do something, that was "talking back". Defending myself being considered talking back would eventually lead me into trouble.

Maria set me on the road to independence early. I was attending Maryland Avenue School on the east side, and that meant that I had to take a bus alone at 7 years old as no one else in my new neighborhood attended that school (this was during a time when most kids attended their neighborhood schools). I loved Maryland Avenue. While I suffered bullying and ridicule, I also discovered my gift of learning there as well.

The morning of my first day, Maria walked me to the bus stop. My house was on one corner and the bus stop was on the other corner across the street. She gestured that when I would exit the bus, I'd simply cross the street and walk home. I thought that I could do it. However, the first day that I came home would prove otherwise. Once I exited the bus, everything looked foreign to me and I just took my little feet and began walking...trying to find something that would indicate where I was. Eventually, Maria realized I should've been home and drove around until she found me. After that, she made sure that I knew how to get home but continued to let me walk back and forth by myself.

By this time, the school had already discovered that I was academically beyond my years, especially in the area of reading. The one accommodation they'd made was to send me to the next level up for reading. Even though I was more advanced than the third graders, they felt I wasn't mature enough to go to the fourth-grade class.

Maryland Avenue was my heart. It was where I felt like a kid. During these days, there were kids from so many backgrounds, races and economic statuses. I envied my white counterparts who walked to school and brought bag lunches every day. One day, I asked my foster mom if I could pack a lunch and she said I could. I packed a sandwich, some chips, cookies, and an apple. I was so proud of my lunch that once I got on the bus that morning, I started to eat it.

I must've had the look of naivete on my face as one of the older kids called me to the back of the bus to sit with them. I knew this kid was no friend and only wanted me for my snacks, but at this stage in the game I had no autonomy over my body or choices. If someone said to come, I came, even if I knew they had ill intent. They told me to sit in the inside seat and asked me if they could tie my shoe. I knew how to tie my shoe as Silvia had taught me one day when she "had had it with tying my shoes," but I didn't even consider saying no. I watched as they took my lunch into their possession, passing treats among friends and taking my shoelaces and tying the left shoe with the right. I didn't flinch or cry as by this time there were so many people who treated me wrong because they felt like it. I just planned to untie my shoes once they were done and before I exited the bus. In terms of my lunch, I was OK with the fact that they ate everything but the sandwich. I knew I still could get the regular lunch. When it came time to untie my shoes, I realized that the knots were so tight that I had to break the shoelaces to get them apart. I pulled apart what I could and cut them with scissors when I was able and went on about my day.

That wasn't my first time being bullied at Maryland Avenue. I was tortured by an upperclassman in a random act of violence in the hallway. I don't remember much of it besides sitting in the principal's office so they could get the facts to suspend my assailant. I just remember walking in the hall and being randomly attacked.

When I reflect on all the bullying I endured, I am often amazed at the amount, frequency and the seemingly randomness of it all. But I know spiritually that I was called to be a leader, an innovator and something rather amazing. This was a trick of the enemy... to deceive my mind into believing that I was nothing of value and therefore I should merely exist and not seek to be anything greater than my given circumstances.

But let me tell you how God works! For every portion of darkness and deceit that Satan throws, God ensures that you're just that more talented, wise, and amazing! I have always been wise and talented but people don't understand what I had to endure to become who I am. I am absolutely grateful for the gifts that God has given. I have learned that people have free will, so while God stops and protects us from many things, when he allows the things to happen: He already has a remedy and a victory. He wouldn't be God if we didn't have free will but despite us being people with all our flaws and hurts that we act on, he is still truly amazing.

Yet my bullying didn't stop at the kids but also involved the staff. At some point there was a rumor about the scar I had in the center of my forehead that I had obtained by some act of violence when I was really young was indeed ringworm. For all the adults that asked I explained that it was a scar. Someone wasn't satisfied and alerted the principal. Therefore, one day as I boarded the bus to go home, the principal made everyone leave the bus so that she could inspect my face. I was humiliated but didn't shed a tear. After she finished examining my face by squinting the eyes of her wide face - a black woman who looked very much like the comedian Luenell, she slithered her huge walrus body out of the seat and declared it wasn't ringworm after all. I am not sure how any of this was legal in the early 90's, but it happened.

During this time, my foster mother's house consisted of her eldest foster daughter, Lyneisha, who was about 9; my 5-year-old sister; Maria's youngest foster daughter Katrice, who was 2; and Maria's two biological children, Sherry, who was 15, and Courtney, who was 8. She also had a live-in boyfriend, Leon, who has the father of her children.

With so many girls in the house from so many backgrounds, the mix was interesting. Sherry was in high school so she wasn't around much. Lyneisha was the oldest of us foster kids but was always in trouble. She prided herself on saying how attractive she was, and Maria created a campaign to let her know she wasn't "all that" and perhaps that is why Lyneisha was so mean to us. Lyneisha once slammed my sister's hand in the window and did her best to make me feel that she was better than me in every way. I loved to sing and people told me I could. Lyneisha also was talented in singing so she did her best to make sure that people agreed she was better.

Lyneisha was constantly bothering me and trying to get me in trouble. There was one time I was sure she had succeeded, but my foster mom threw us both for a loop. Sometimes as a consequence we'd be sent to bed early. That meant that we might not get dinner. Well, I wrote about this time I was sent to bed early in my diary where I described stealing a piece of bologna out of the refrigerator and hiding it in my underwear until I made it back to my room. Lyneisha couldn't wait to divulge this information during one of her tattle moments. However, she ended up getting in trouble for reading my private moments (no pun intended).

As we got older, the more divided we became. Lyneisha and I were never friends, and my sister was my sister. Katrice though a foster child just like us clearly had a different relationship than we did.

For one thing, Katrice was sent to Maria's house as a baby so there was a different dynamic and bond created. She also was like a daughter to Maria's oldest daughter, Stacy, who was already an adult and out of the house by the time we moved in.

The first few Christmases were a dream. We'd have to go to sleep and at some point during the night/early morning, a bag of toys was placed at the ends of our beds. Each person had a bag exploding with toys. I was a light sleeper so every time Maria did this, I'd hop up as soon as she went downstairs! The expectation was that we would play with our gifts and thank her once she came back up later that day.

However as we got older, that Christmas tradition began to change. There was one Christmas in particular that Maria told us we weren't getting anything. She let us know early on she was "muthafuckin' Santa Claus" and we weren't getting anything. Despite her words, I didn't believe her. Traditionally at midnight we'd pretend to be asleep as she left us each a garbage bag full of toys and when I was younger, even though she said she was "muthafuckin' Santa Claus" I still believed he existed. There were nights I'd pretend to sleep and open my eyes quickly to see if I caught him in the window. This was despite all the Christmas' before with no gift. I am not sure why I believed in that man despite him not showing up for me many times.

So that Christmas night, we didn't receive our bags of gifts but in my heart I knew she was just pulling our leg. The next morning, she reminded us that she'd told us we weren't getting anything and she meant it. That is when emptiness set in. Yet just as I was getting ready to have no hope she told us she had a dollar waiting for us downstairs. We all climbed over each other in order to get down stairs first knowing we had more than a dollar waiting. Yet when we arrived we saw a large mound of presents for Katrice and we indeed got a dollar. The end. That was our Christmas that year. I watched Katrice bask in the feeling of being loved and breathed in what it was like to not be us.

Things weren't all bad in the Miller household. Maria did affirm me at this age. She'd tell me how smart I was and that one day I'd be able to outsmart her. She'd let me read to her and when she tired of that, she'd tell me to read to her dolls or to Courtney. She nurtured the love of reading in me by placing me in a book club that sent me books every month. I owned a series titled: " The Adventures of Spike and Mike". It was about an alligator and a bird whose eggs landed in the same nest during a rainstorm. Once they opened they became instant siblings and you couldn't tell them anything!

She also provided family fun sometimes. One time, she left the younger children with family and she and her boyfriend surprised the older kids with a trip to Six Flags. This is when I learned that roller coasters and I weren't compatible. Also she'd sometimes pull out the board games and we'd play games like pochino as a family.

While I wasn't the oldest , I was the most mature so when Maria had quick runs to make, she'd ask me to watch Courtney. Sometimes it was as simple as sleeping in Maria's water bed while she was gone to make sure Courtney was safe or simply being present to make sure all was well with Courtney. Courtney required timely feedings and diaper changes, so Maria never stayed gone long as she took very good care of Courtney and I wasn't responsible for those tasks. Despite that, one day she came home with gifts. I was so shocked and excited. When I asked her why, she said it was a gift for taking such good care of Courtney. I was excited for my pencil cup holder and other knick knacks because I didn't know I could earn anything simply for doing what I was told.

The magic of innocence was still very much a part of my childhood. Every Saturday, we went to The Boys and Girls Club. I loved the club! All of the staff were kind and you made your own schedule. If you wanted to do art at 1 p.m. and go to the game room at 3, that's what you did! That is where I met people like Carla Jackson, who would support my writing of poetry and offer me my first job, to Frankie (RIP), who was a no-nonsense boss who also was sweet and easy to talk to. I'd also be remiss to not mention LaQuita, who nurtured everyone's love for books and had such a patient nature. We had an amazing computer room attendant named Amanda who later blessed me on my first Christmas as an independent "woman" with things on my wish list. There was so much love and support that I found at the Boys and Girls Club!

The Boys and Girls Club would be where I put my first dance class together, and we'd be given a boombox and be able to create a routine in the hallway. There was always fun, contests, and prizes. I hope that same spirit lives in the cubs today as it brought so much magic and joy into our lives.

Even at the Boys and Girls Club, people saw me as an individual. For a brief stint, a lady by the name of Monica took me under her wing and gave me some one-on-one time. We'd go to church, talk for hours while she was at work, and she'd give me advice. Wherever and whenever there was a lack at home, God always had a ram in the bush. There was somebody who God was using to let me know that I mattered.

The Boys and Girls Club was a drive Maria didn't always want to take because it was about 20 minutes into the city. The summer days when she didn't feel like driving, we'd have what was called recreation in the park. In the 90's, schools were safe havens even during the summer. My elementary school had a small building that was the grounds of the school park and that opened for the summer. They had a scheduled lunch time, games, and more. Though the Boys and Girls Club was unmatched, we were OK with this alternative.

One summer there was a family that moved into the neighborhood that loved to cause trouble. Before I knew it, I was in a physical fight with one of the girls where we had our fair share of "licks" given. The worst of that fight was that I somehow ended up with several pieces of a prickly plant in my nose. The instigator was sent home, and I pulled the thorns out of my nose and went on with my day.

However, there was a fight to come that summer that didn't end so quickly. This same family decided that my friends and I were targets of their verbal abuse. We were not going to be outdone so we came back with the threats of violence. One of the family members said that they had some cousins they could go get and then "it was on." While they were gone, my friends and I decided to go on top of the tot lot and throw rocks as they came toward us. So we spent the next 10 minutes gathering rocks to throw and we climbed to the top of the tot lot. Even though that plan seemed foolproof, that is not what actually happened.

When my friends and sister saw how many people our neighbors brought back (at least 20) they threw a few rocks and then they all began to run. It was myself, and my friends Jennifer and Jessica who were left behind. Jennifer placed Jessica on her bike and they were off! I caught up and asked to hop on. Jennifer balanced Jessica on front and me on back for a short while before she let me know that I had to get off. I was about two blocks from my house when one of the boys involved spotted me and chased me all the way home. I beat him to my door where I started banging and ringing the doorbell. My foster mother arrived right before his foot hit the porch. Seeing him gesture himself toward me, my foster mother let him know that he wasn't to touch me. She stood in between the boy and me. He kept trying to get around her saying "Ma'am, just let me handle this. She shouldn't have been throwing rocks at my cousins." My foster mother let him know that it didn't matter what I did, he wasn't going to touch me.

By this time, an older family member of the boy arrived and made the boy come with him. He apologized to my foster mother for the disrespect and dragged the boy home. Of course I was in trouble, but I didn't care. I thought I was going to lose my life that day, but she protected me and I believe she would've fought the boy if he went through with his threats.

One thing about my foster mother was that she had the strong black women down to a science. One day she told me that she had to leave town for a few days to pay her respects to a family member who passed. So we'd be divided up among her family until she came back. I was sent to stay with her cousin Linda. I hadn't really known Linda prior to that but I had the best experience with her. That was the first time I felt "spoiled". Linda let me play in the basement and pick things I wanted from the grocery store. I didn't have any responsibilities to anyone. Linda also was the only relative that would be honest with my foster mom when she mistreated us. Everyone else took Maria's lead and if we were nothing to her, we were invisible to them.

When Maria returned, it was as if nothing happened. I never saw her shed a tear. There was once during that period where someone was being behaviorally challenging and she reminded us that she was grieving. It wasn't too long later that she revealed that she had breast cancer and opted to have the tumors removed. Again, she never missed a beat. She was always strong, but I think her strength sometimes made her cold.

The green and white house on the corner that we lived in had a dark secret of its own: It was haunted, and it didn't take long for me to figure this out. There were doors that would slam in the distance and things I'd see move out of the corner of my eye. One night Maria came upstairs to see what all the commotion she heard late at night was about to only discover we were all asleep! Right in my bedroom...in my bed, was the sound of someone jumping. Out of pure shock and curiosity she woke my sister and myself up and had us switch beds to see if the jumping would stop. The jumper followed me right to my sister's bed, and I lay awake tortured by the sound of this supernatural experience. One thing Maria didn't mind was TV time. Therefore I was able to watch TV until I fell asleep.

Eventually, Lyneisha moved back in with her biological mother and Tarsha joined us. My sister and Tarsha became instant best friends. They had similar names, were the same age and had birthdays that were only a couple weeks apart! They told everyone they were fraternal twins and many of their friends believed them as if it made sense.

Maria loved Tarsha from inception. One of the first things Tarsha did was clean her closet and Maria was so captivated by having a daughter who loved to clean. I was annoyed by all of the attention Tarsha got and the pedestal they put her on. To make matters worse, though Tarsha was 3 years younger than me, we were close to the same size so to start Tarsha off, Maria took a bunch of my clothes that she deemed too small and gave them to Tarsha. There were some that were too small but not everything. The one thing that hurt me the most was when she took my raincoat and gave it to Tarsha and left me with a poncho. It was better to wear no raincoat than to wear a poncho in elementary school so when it rained, I cried because Tarsha had my raincoat and left me looking like a homeless person (in my eyes and the eyes of my classmates if I was bold enough to wear that in school).

Tarsha was sweet as she could be but I didn't like how she was treated better than me so I didn't really like her. Tarsha had been with us a brief amount of time when Stacy, Maria's oldest daughter, took Tarsha and I over for a visit to her house as she sometimes did. This particular day she had her friend Marquita's daughter over, and I told Marquita that we would play without Tarsha and that is what we did until Tarsha told on us. When Stacy asked me why I excluded Tarsha, I explained that I wanted something to myself as Tarsha was getting treated better than me. Stacy told me that that wasn't true and asked Tarsha, "Do you think you get treated better than everyone else" and she replied , "Yes." Instead of Stacy taking a look at both her and her mother's practices, she chuckled, told Tarsha that that wasn't true and restricted me from playing with them. I now was partaking in the very ritual I was afraid of. My heart was broken.

Ch.5

ADVENTURES OF A YOUNG TEEN

My teenage years were extremely depressing. It was the season in my life when I contemplated sucide frequently. Two things that stopped me from going through with it. One was I had watched a TV show where a child was missing part of his skull where he was shot in the head. I decided that if I lived, I didn't want lasting effects. Plus, I didn't want my suicide to be violent. I also had a healthy balance of good days.

Home life used to drive me insane. I could never do right even when I did right. She said that I couldn't do dance at school nor would she pay for me to take dance classes. She said that eventually I could but I needed to wait so I accepted it. She told me to be home at a certain time, I was. I had to watch the kids (her young niece and nephew came to live with us. Dion was 3 or 4 and Lin'e was 6 or 7) every day, and I did it while doing my homework.

I was not the best at doing chores. It wasn't that I intentionally half did them but it was that I did not give my full effort. There were times that I was up late after the kids had gone to bed doing homework and I was told "fuck your homework...come clean the kitchen." I was told when we were in cahoots that I put salt in her sugar, intentionally coughed when I walked past her cooking or that I broke the washing machine. I was tired of being blamed for things that I wouldn't even fathom doing. There was one time my foster sister Tarsha wrote on HER window sill in HER room , "I Hate Momma"and I was blamed for it. When I explained that it was misspelled and written in Tarsha's penmanship instead of my foster mom admitting she was wrong, she said I was trying to frame Tarsha. I couldn't defend myself because that was considered talking back and she would rip up the letters I would write pleading for her to see me differently. Those things broke my heart!

Middle school was rough for me. I started out at John Burroughs Middle School. I had two black teachers who seemed to be best friends, Ms. Lee and Ms. Bailey. They were in sync with each other and worked in tandem to provide us all a very rich educational experience. They were 20-something-year-old teachers who made learning fun. Ms. Bailey was tall, light-skinned and had freckles on her cheeks. I always thought she dressed the cutest and of the two she was the laid-back one. Ms. Lee was light-skinned, short, had a short haircut and was so beautiful to me. I had a secret obsession with Ms. Lee! I wanted her to love me so bad, to be one of her favorites and find me to be special. While Ms. Lee was kind and loving to everyone, I never got to be her favorite pick.

I'll never forget how much she adored my classmate Christina. Christina was the one who ran her errands, who got to sit by her when we were having talent show rehearsals and one whom she'd laugh with. I used to rack my brain trying to see what made Christina special and I came up with every scenario. Was it because both of their first names had many letters? Was it because Christina's hair was long? Was she prettier than me? I didn't know what it was but all I wanted to do was figure it out so that I could be loved like Christina!

As always, my life wouldn't be complete without bullies and I had several that year alone. My first bully was a girl by the name of Carla. Carla was a light-skinned tall girl who was a bit on the chunky side. She wore her hair in a short wrap and was pretty popular. For whatever reason, she'd always say mean things to me. I'd go home and my foster mother would listen and eventually she said, "The next time she bothers you... beat her ass." I wasn't looking forward to fighting Carla but I was excited about not getting in trouble for fighting.

That was basically all the ammunition I needed! The image is clear as if it was yesterday. We were in reading class supposed to be having independent reading time ...even the teacher was reading. I tapped the boy sitting next to me whose name was D'Angelo and I said, "I'm about to hit Carla." He said, "Let me see." So I got up to pretend to sharpen my pencil, walked past her desk and went back to my seat and chickened out. D'Angelo turned to me and said, "I knew you were lying."

At that point, I had to save face so with all the strength I had, I did the same move but when I got to her desk, I stabbed her with the newly sharpened pencil on her shoulder. Imagine the yelp in her voice as she leaped up from the book she was reading. She was fuming and we began to exchange blows. The desks were in nice neat rows which worked in my favor because eventually I got loose and I started to run from her. At some point, I picked up a garbage can to defend myself but by that time, the teacher had intervened and I was headed to the principal's office. The teacher actually came to my defense as she didn't know who hit who first. She said she concluded that Carla hit me first as she had seen her bully me many times before. I proudly let her know that no, I was the perpetrator for that very reason. I was tired of being bullied and my mama said I could defend myself. We were both suspended but that was the first time, suspension was a happy occasion.

Carla wasn't the last. There was Jena who bullied me on the bus until we went to blows. This time I was stronger and gave her what I wanted to give to so many that came before. Eventually the bus stopped and we exchanged blow for blow. That would be the last time she bullied me!

Sixth grade was an eye-opener for me. I was shocked by how many kids would smoke weed right outside the schoolhouse door before we'd go inside. They were never penalized and they didn't hide their deeds! I know I stuck out like a sore thumb as I was trying my best to be invisible. I wasn't afraid of the temptation as I wasn't the least bit interested but I was afraid of the harassment. I had no entourage. I just wanted to be left alone. I wanted only to be noticed by people who cared to lift me up, see me and love me authentically. Those situations weren't free for the taking but I always dreamed...hoped for the possibility.

Interesting enough, the journey to school was a rough one! I think about how my daughters who are growing up in suburbia bus comes to the end of the block and though all the kids in the neighborhood live within blocks of each other, all of them get the same treatment..their bus goes from corner to corner! I never knew it was a thing!

I had to walk several blocks to my bus stop and enter a neighborhood (though only about six blocks away) that was much more dangerous than my own. It was on a busy street so I had to look like, "Fuck you looking at?" (I am not an advocate of profanity and don't use it regularly... I use these words to explain the severity of the look) to deter any man (and they were mostly men) from thinking I was an easy target or wanted to be talked to at all! In addition to that, my foster mother told me that gang activity was heavy in that area so I had to be mindful of the clothes I wore so as to not rep a set. I was scared and mostly alone as that's when kids started to not really go to school. So while there were about three other people who shared the bus stop, 60% of the time I was there alone! Sometimes I'd be so surprised to see some of my bus stop pals as so much time had passed, I swore they had changed schools.

Getting to and through middle school was a whole ordeal and I lived in my head a lot! This is the age where I made clear lines in the sand about who I wanted to be. I wasn't having sex. I didn't want a boyfriend. I wanted to be the best student I could be for myself. I wanted good friends who wanted to do good things. I was very clear and very strong on these things and I truly believe in spiritual warfare. I believe that I was attacked physically so much because I was the child of promise and therefore people were a part of the mission to abort my destiny and they didn't even know they were doing it! They probably just thought that they didn't like me and they didn't know why. And while I had my priorities in order of my do's and don'ts I was still broken and lacked self-esteem. What I had was self worth and though they are related they were not the same.

Low self-esteem showed up in how I dealt with my hygiene. In elementary school, I had shoulder-length hair and I remember several girls playing with it when we had free time or "Fun Friday," but in the fifth grade, around the middle of the year, my hair began to break off. Initially it wasn't so bad. That was the first time my foster mother took me to the shop (beauty salon) to get my hair done. She got it braided in two french braids with weave attached. When I came to school, everyone assumed it was mine and I adorned it with hairballs at the end and I was happy. However once those braids came out, my relaxed hair began to fall out everytime I combed it. I thought it was shedding but when my hair began to get patchy, I knew that it was more serious than I originally understood.

At this point my foster mother sent me to her friend's daughter who was a braiding wizard. She also had other interests and since I was a kid, attention to detail wasn't most important to her. She became my hair braider and that is how I got through that stage without much bullying. She would place my hair in box braids about shoulder length mostly in medium/large fashion. While she knew the width of them would make them not last as long, she'd do them this size because she just wanted to get it finished. They were neat but my foster mother and I knew that within weeks, they'd need to be redone and she wasn't paying to have them refreshed that often.

Also in the earliest stages of this process, my hair had broken off so badly that she could not add braids to the lower-back section of my hair. So to mask this, I had all the other braids pulled back in a ponytail to hide this section. It camouflaged pretty well or at least I thought but we were in lines at this age and I'll never forget when

Raynette pulled my ponytail up and asked me what happened in the back. I tried to play it cool and said, "Oh she didn't get to that section yet" and her response was "How can she?" The jig was up. There were so many girls with hair deficiencies that I didn't get picked on too much about it. It was actually as if they were relieved that I was one of them and they didn't have to envy my hair any more. This was the same girl who months ago would play in my hair and tell me how long it was and now she had a ball headed ponytail while I had a bush of hair in the back and strands of length here and there in the front.

The good news is the extreme baldness didn't last long but once it was long enough to manage, I was responsible for managing it between braids. That hurt my feelings because everyone else in the house had long, thick hair and they still were able to get their hair combed but my hair was a nuisance that I had to deal with on my own.

By the time I got to middle school, I had come into styling my hair and not feeling so much pity about it. There were so many times it looked ridiculous. We still wore balls and barrettes so I tried my best to make it work. I tried braiding it into a ponytail, making a smooth ponytail etc. My foster mother had also decided that since relaxers damaged my hair so badly, she'd only lightly relax it with what she called a "kiddie perm". What that meant is that I would get my hair relaxed with a relaxer designed for prepubescent children and at the first sign of burning, she'd wash it out even if it wasn't straight. Therefore my hair never broke off as severely as it did in fifth grade but between me trying to flat-iron it, curl it, braid it with no guidance, it stayed in a damaged state and the only time my hair actually looked good was when I was able to get my braids put in.

This coupled with feeling very alone in the world and having no one to trust with my feelings made me have low self-esteem. I knew I was smart but that was all I had. I didn't feel pretty and I couldn't dress well.

I distinctly remember being so proud of my new sweatshirt one wintery sixth grade morning. It was neon yellow with a green alien on it in the middle of the shirt with his arms crossed. Above the alien was a halo and words that read "I'm no angel." That same day, the ribbing sessions began, and I was drafted as something to laugh at. This time I played it pretty cool but hearing, "Yo' shirt so bright, you light up the room" was enough for me. That sweatshirt went to the back of the closet and I never wore it again!

Home life for the most part was a drag. My foster mother would come and go as she pleased and demanded that the younger kids be watched. I was the oldest and was responsible for keeping things in order. At this time, it was my younger sister, my foster sister, and my foster mother's very young niece and nephew who came to stay with us. On occasion, she'd have me watch her special needs daughter (who was definitely a sister to me) but most times she'd take her with her or her father would have her downstairs with him.

I wasn't paid much attention and I didn't pay much attention to myself, either. We also had some plumbing issues in our bathroom, so sometimes, we had to pour hot water in the bathtub and sometimes we'd have a bucket in the sink that we'd fill with water to either bathe in or wash our hands then we'd pour the bucket out. So many times I would forgo bathing and do a quick wash up, not paying attention to detail, and it showed. I definitely was musty many days in middle school.

So there came parent-teacher conferences and my grades were fine so there was nothing of concern there. Yet Ms. Lee and Ms. Bailey asked for me to step out of the room and I was nervous of why they needed me to leave. I had a yelling issue. Was it that?

I was at the "bottle it all up inside and explode" stage. Looking back, I wish someone cared enough to see me then. I was so full of rage from all the bullying, responsibilities at home, name calling, unwarranted pinches, etc. The way my rage showed up was extreme. I was somewhat social in the classroom but when kids continually said things that bothered me, I would bottle it up and scream at them. There was this time when Ms. Lee asked us all to bring a green notebook to class because she wanted to retire our binders. I kept forgetting to ask my foster mom to give me one (as she had stacks of school supplies in her room). Ms. Lee did her due diligence to remind us but I was so forgetful. Well one day, a student asked her why we hadn't started using our notebooks and she said, " oh someone hasn't brought theirs in yet." When they asked her who, she didn't say my name but she looked in my area and my face must've told it all because they started to say things like "Ugh...why haven't you brought your notebook in? It's your fault we can't work in them." Well that day was "explode day" so I yelled, "LEAVE ME ALONE! I FORGOT!" Anytime I got like that, Ms. Lee would call security but I'd be calm by the time they came and she'd just gesture them away. I didn't explode like that all the time, but I certainly did it a few times and it was always in Ms. Lee's class.

I had several interesting occurrences in Ms. Lee's class that year. Ms. Lee taught social studies and we were doing a unit on transportation. She told us to bring in supplies and we would work on modes of transportation both at home and in school. I was so excited! I stole our pasta from home that was shaped like wheels,and took a shoebox and other random supplies. I was crafting my vehicle with one hand on the bottom of the box and the other puncturing the box with a pair of scissors. Before I knew it those scissors went through the top of the box to the bottom. I had stabbed myself. I was so freaked out that I hid my bleeding finger underneath my desk hoping it would stop bleeding after a few drops. I did a great job hiding my middle finger on my left hand (which I remember because I used my dominant hand to stab myself) until Johnathan Bradley, the class clown, came over to bother me as he did on a daily basis. While Johnathan had his fair share of talking about people which he did do, his teasing was different. He wasn't malicious, though it could be hurtful, he just wanted a laugh.

I'll never forget how we were in Ms. Lee's class while she was teaching math and Johnathan was singing Dionne Farris' "Hopeless" song but the original lyrics go "They say I'm hopeless...like a penny with a hole in it." However, for whatever reason, Jonathan kept singing, "They say I'm holey...like a sweater with a hole in it" and everyone was laughing. It took me a while to realize that it was because he was making fun of the most quiet student in class, Kaying, who happened to have a small hole in her sweater. I will admit that I laughed. It was even more funny because she had no clue that Johnathan was not just singing a song or if she did, her face didn't show it all.

So when he came over to my desk as I was trying to hide my finger, I did my best to let him say his witty and rude comments but of course he noticed my finger as by this time, there was a puddle of blood on the floor. He asked me why I didn't get a band-aid, and he went to tell Ms. Lee who immediately sent me to the bathroom to wash my finger. I tried for several minutes to stop the bleeding and then I wrapped my finger and went back to the room. There, Ms. Lee gave me a band-aid and looked at my finger and said, "Your finger should've stopped bleeding by now. Your blood isn't clotting. You may have to go to the hospital." Now why did she say that to me? She had me terrified I was going to lose my finger. However, not too long after I placed the band-aid on my finger, the bleeding finally stopped.

Now what happened the next day embarrassed me and hurt my feelings. I was on a high from yesterday because Ms. Lee and I shared a moment when she examined my finger. That small time when I mattered was everything to me. One because it was Ms. Lee but even more because there wasn't any individual attention happening at home. Yet as I started my day at my locker Ms. Lee came out to get me. She had a sponge, a bucket of water and Ajax waiting for me and she told me that I had to clean up my blood. I don't know why that hurt my feelings as there wasn't anything wrong with the request (it was just a little off because we had janitors) but I guess it felt more like a punishment. As I examine it now as an adult who has been seeing a therapist, I can say it probably brought me back to my original thought from when I hid my bleeding finger. Her having me clean up my blood made me feel as if I was getting punished for hurting myself...like I wasn't good enough to be hurt so here was my consequence for crossing that line.

In the process of cleaning up my blood, I overestimated the amount of Ajax that I needed and poured a massive amount on the floor. When Ms. Lee noticed she stopped me and said, "Nun unh...what you doing, you don't know how to clean? That's too much!" She wasn't mean about it, she was just matter of fact and that's when she called the janitor to finish the job as I made the situation worse.

As I stated, sixth grade was rough and it didn't end there. I was going through a hair battle and I noticed this girl Tenisha had a Jheri curl and she went from really short hair to hair that was growing. I came home one day and asked my foster mom for a Jheri curl and to my surprise, she obliged. She felt that it was a healthy medium between relaxers and my natural hair that would sweat out the next day after getting it pressed. So she set me up with the same hairdresser who had put the two weave braids in my hair a year ago and told her the style I wanted. Marla applied the texturizer and rollers and I was excited until she took out the clippers and proceeded to shave the sides of my hair. I cried and cried. Marla didn't flinch as she said it would be a cute hair cut. I didn't understand why she wanted me to look like a boy. I also didn't understand why she wanted such a grown-up hairstyle on a 12-year-old girl. My foster mother also was disappointed when she came to pick me up and told Marla that she shouldn't have shaved my sides if I didn't ask. So as asked, I had a Jheri curl but it wasn't anything like Tenisha's.

My Jheri curl, or wave nouveau as I was told it was called, stayed dry! I'd leave the shop with tight bouncy curls and about a minute after I removed my cap, my hair would be dry. I begin to pack my gel and spray as preventative measures. When I say my hair dried fast, I mean that. There was this time I was on the bus, sitting close to the front in order to avoid being bullied. My hair was dry and I couldn't take out my products as I'd get laughed at so I used the bus driver's mirror to spit in my hair in hopes to give it the moisture it needed. What I didn't know was that just like I could see in the mirror, others could see me and boy did I get talked about that day! I was the "girl who spit in her hair."

Despite getting talked about I still believed in myself and my talents. That spring, John Burroughs put on a talent show and I wanted to audition. Ms. Lee was in charge of keeping everyone's music so I brought my Aaliyah tape to play in the background as I sang. I unfortunately was not selected to perform in the talent show but I had to wait until she gave everyone back their music in order to get mine as she would have to sift through it. During this time, Carla came to me and said that she noticed that I gave Ms. Lee my Aaliyah tape and could she have it. I told her no. Remember, Carla was the same girl I fought at the beginning of the year. While we were on fine terms, I wanted my Aaliyah tape! Well when it came time to return merchandise I never got my tape back, and I knew who had stolen it. Yet I didn't want to burden Ms. Lee with the fact that she hadn't protected my merchandise so I never mentioned it and just counted my losses and dealt with my sadness and disappointment privately.

Year 12 wasn't only rough at school but also at home. My foster mother had very strict rules about what it meant to talk back and that meant even if you were defending yourself, that was a form of disrespect. So around my birthday I was on punishment and that meant there would be no party. Having no party was probably something I could've lived with but I received no acknowledgement that I aged it all. I felt 100% empty inside on my 12th birthday especially because I was a good kid! I didn't talk back, I was compliant, got good grades solely on my own strength, etc. But whatever I did/was accused of did not warrant that feeling of no love I received. During this time my mother and father weren't in my life and her family only acknowledged us when we were around so there was no one to make me feel valuable that year. To make matters worse when I went to school, the kids asked me why they didn't see any of my birthday stuff as they knew my day had passed recently and before I could lie someone jokingly said, "Well, she has some new barrettes so I think she got them for her birthday." As humiliating as that was, I was relieved to not be seen as a liar because I wasn't going to let my peers know that I didn't even get a "happy birthday" on my birthday.

Ms. Lee and Ms. Bailey were rebels when it came to educating us. One thing that they didn't like was that we didn't have recess. They felt that at our age and development, we still needed recess. So sometimes they'd randomly divide the kids up and one would keep the students who had behavior issues and the other teacher would take the kids who were behaving outside for some free time. I imagine that one teacher also stayed in to keep watch in case the administration found out. Well, this day my choices led to unintentionally exposing what Ms. Lee and Ms. Bailey were doing for us.

I am the queen of double-dutch. To this day, I don't know anyone who can jump longer than me or do as many tricks. Our recess time started off like any other time until someone brought out the ropes. It was my turn to jump, and I took off my shoes because the best jumping comes from when you can feel your feet on the earth. Well when I came down from one of my spin moves, I landed on my foot. My feet sometimes lean on the side so I jumped on top of the side of my foot that was leaning over and fractured my foot.

I heard the crack and I felt the break. I was confident that my foot was broken because I had broken the opposite foot the year before doing the exact same thing.

Well just like the scissors incident, I got quiet. I didn't shed a tear. I just found somewhere to sit and told the kids I was no longer interested in playing. I played everything cool until it was time to go in and I could barely walk. It brought me back to when I was in fifth grade and I broke my foot outside the house.

In fifth grade, at first I didn't know my foot was broken. It hurt and my foster mother wasn't home at the time so I hopped on one foot up the stairs to silently deal with my pain. She discovered my foot was broken because she called me downstairs and I took forever to arrive. When I made it downstairs she was livid until she saw my face. She asked me what took me so long and when I told her what happened, she said she knew something was up because I never took that long to come and do what she asked me.

Having a broken foot at school and home was fun at first. People would take my tray and get lunch and I was relieved of some of the chores at home. My foster mother even drove me to school each day. Yet just like most things where I felt special and cared for, that was short-lived. After about two weeks, my foster mother who had no job or appointments in the morning told me that I would now walk the five blocks to my elementary school on crutches. There were two busy streets I had to cross in addition to three other streets to get to school. I was crushed and embarrassed! After the shock wore off and my siblings began to walk to school, I pushed myself to try to move as quickly as they did even with crutches.

I guess the impact was too much and my wooden crutches broke about halfway into our trek. I had to hop all the way home on one leg. My foster mother wasn't outdone, however. She went to a neighbor friend who had just gotten off crutches and asked to borrow them. My foster mother was confident in her crutches as hers were metal, and I continued my walk to school.

So as I came to grips that this was happening again and that I would be in trouble as I wasn't supposed to jump double-dutch ever again (my foster mother felt that it was possible to break my foot again... and here we were) ... I went within myself. Because I was moving so slowly and kids really liked to push at this time, I let my classmates know my foot was broken. They became extremely concerned and told Ms. Lee. Ms. Lee told me that it couldn't be broken because I could walk and I wasn't crying and because it was Ms. Lee and I thought the world of her, I didn't dare argue. I made it back to class and Ms. Lee announced that we were going to the computer lab to do research. Why did she say that? I let her know that I wasn't going to make it. She gave me a pass and sent me to Ms. Bailey's room.

Ms. Bailey asked me what happened and helped me to the computer desk near the front of the room. She began to teach her class and I began to feel excruciating pain. At this point, I put my head in my arms and cried quietly. I stayed at that computer table until the end of the day (which was only an hour or so) and that is when Ms. Lee and Ms. Bailey realized that we had a bigger problem: I couldn't walk.

Ms. Lee's theory about my lack of pain and being able to walk was partially true as I know I wasn't able to put weight on my broken foot. They dismissed all the students and dragged their feet to the principal's office to get help as they knew they'd have to tell about the secret recess. Mr. Brazil was a tall no-nonsense man who came back with my teachers and a wheelchair! I was mortified! One of my reasons was because I imagined myself sitting in that wheelchair and the whole school pointing and laughing as I boarded the bus. As silly as that image seems now, it seemed very real back then. The three of them begged me to get in a wheelchair and I refused. They then held my bus and found a girl named Sharia who was this tall, dark-skinned, heavyset girl who lived in my neighborhood. She agreed to allow me to lean on her as I hopped with my good foot. The problem was she wanted to walk really fast and when I told her that she was doing that, she got mad and gave up.

By this time, Ms. Lee, Ms. Bailey and the principal had left for the day and assumed I went with Sharia. Sharia left me, too. So there I sat in the middle of the hallway thinking about how I was going to move. Once I saw that the coast was clear, I crawled to the front of the school and sat on a window ledge. For about an hour I listened to sounds. I zeroed in on every after-school program and every conversation I could hear. I was also consumed with worry of how I was going to get home.

After school let out, an assistant principal noticed I was still there and helped me to her office. She began frantically calling my house and leaving messages. After about 30 minutes she said , "Look...they're gonna have to pick you up from outside. I have a doctor's appointment that I can't miss because he's booked for months." So she helped me outside and left me at school alone sitting on the concrete. I eventually pulled myself onto my backpack and made myself a seat.

There I sat for quite a bit of time with not one fear but in complete shock when my foster mother's van pulled up and she and her boyfriend got out. By this time, she had heard the messages and brought him along as she knew she needed help carrying me. They lifted me into the car and asked me what happened and why I wasn't crying. She dropped him off and we went to the ER where I was informed that I had fractured my foot in two places. My foster mother put her foot down that day and said that I definitely could never jump double-dutch again.

Returning to school the next day was interesting! Ms. Lee and Ms. Bailey were extremely nice to me. They made sure someone always pulled me up a chair and that I had any physical support I needed. I later learned that I had every right to sue the school and that they were pretty nervous about it all. Like all other trauma in my life, I eventually healed and the cast was removed. I had a strong desire to jump as soon as the cast was removed but I knew I couldn't. I even tried once when the neighborhood kids asked me to play double dutch. My foster mother said I could turn but I couldn't jump. Well I moved our game across the street where I thought she couldn't see and had myself a good time jumping. I was mortified when she called me in as soon as I was done. I remember praying and hoping she wanted something else but she called me in to tell me she saw me, I now was forbidden from playing the game at all and I had to stay in the rest of the day. I had a deep lump in my chest. I was so salty and sad.

Around the same time my classmates were slated to go to camp. My foster mother decided those consequences weren't enough for me and she called my teachers and told them to use the money she paid to send someone else to camp. I was so hurt and I begged her to have a change of mind but her mind was made up. In addition to that, I had to spend three days with the seventh graders while my classmates enjoyed camp. It was a deeper cut when they came back discussing all their adventures. It was one thing to not go to camp with my friends and classmates but it was a whole other thing to not have an opportunity to have fun with Ms. Lee. I wanted so desperately to share a laugh with her as to convince her to make me one of her favorites yet that chance was forfeited. I remember trying to figure out who was able to go to camp on my behalf and in my head it was the poor girl who decided to go close to the last minute. I hated her... I told myself, "She thinks she's all that...how dare she use my money to go camping..."

Despite all I had to endure, I enjoyed having Ms. Bailey and Ms. Lee as my teachers and I was so sad it had to end. I was so upset at the thought that Ms. Lee would be giving her attention to another group of students.

When seventh grade came, I was hoping for better results as I knew people and I even considered certain people my friends. Back then it was Carmen, Ashley and Keshena who I liked and got along with. We all had our separate friends but we generally enjoyed each other's company and talked on the phone nightly.

So imagine my shock when none of those students were in my class nor any of my classmates. I did, however, inherit some amazing new teachers. There was Ms. Lewis, Ms. Yarn and Mr. Nichols. I'll never forget Mr. Nichols' introduction. He basically said that we'd learn a lot, have a lot of fun but bullying was unequivocally unacceptable. This was the first time I felt protected by a man, and he meant every word. Therefore people reserved their bullying for the other classes.

Ms. Lewis and Ms. Yarn co-taught math and the first days we sat where we wanted. However they eventually sat us next to whom they wanted us by and I was selected to sit next to Courtney Ellis whom I knew from fifth grade. When I sat next to her she created a big fuss as if she didn't know me and started to talk about me. She assumed that since I was quiet I wouldn't say anything back but I had learned to defend myself. She said something about my appearance and I said, "I know you ain't talking with those big, fat Bubbalicious lips" and whatever she was chewing came to a halt and she didn't make another snide comment.

Class with Ms. Lewis and Ms. Yarn was extremely remedial and I explained all these concepts I'd learned in the fourth grade. We started the year reviewing multiplication facts and I was bored but they said so many of us didn't know our facts so we'd all practice together so we could get everyone on the same level. We'd sing a song as a means to practice, " 2, 4, 6, 8 who do we appreciate? Ms. Lewis ...Ms. Yarn... 10, 12, 14, 16 who do we appreciate? Ms. Lewis... Ms. Yarn and we'd replace those numbers for multiples of 3 etc. The problem was most students couldn't do any facts besides 2's, 5's and 9's, so when it was just me and the teachers chanting, the students hated me even more.

It was maybe two weeks into the year and my foster mother had enough with me coming home complaining and she did a surprise pop in and the assistant principal called me in the office. He listened intently and told my foster mom that he wanted to address the bullies strategically so as to not give them any clue as to who told on them to hopefully detour more bullying. My foster mother did not like that plan as she said it doesn't matter if they know just deal with them. Then in a snap decision she said, "I'm tired of this school" and unenrolled me. As I packed up my locker and headed to the car she said, "Imma send you with the white folks 'cause you and black people clearly don't get along." I played it cool and didn't say anything because she defended me but I actually liked the assistant principal's plan and was sad to go because I really liked my teachers, especially Mr. Nichols.

I transferred to Kosciuszko Middle School which was on South Beecher street and had a predominantly hispanic population. I don't know if that's what she meant by white or if that was the closest she could get during that time of the year. I was extremely nervous to attend Kosciuszko and now my commute to school was even longer and scarier! I walked from 5th and Melvina to 11th and Capitol everyday to ride the bus. This was about a 10-block walk over several busy streets that took at minimum 15 minutes to get there.

However, my transition was pretty smooth, and I made some black girl friends rather quickly. My first friend was Lilene Frank. Lilene was very thin, with short, relaxed hair, and she was strikingly beautiful. Like me, Lilene loved to sing and could sing well yet unlike me Lilene was very good with makeup and clothes. That didn't matter and we enjoyed each other's company.

That first year at Kosciuszko was very different from Burroughs. I was bullied far less often and had deeper friendships. There were some hiccups, however. I started band class with a no-nonsense band teacher. I tried to crack a few jokes and was kicked out the same day. That landed me in choir and animation class. That turned out to be an amazing experience! We created commercials, learned how to make clay animations and even sang at the mall and for the local cable station! I even created dance moves for the school song (an adaptation of the popular song "Eye of the Tiger").

I had my first fight at Kosciuszko in that class. We had a substitute teacher and she told us we could have a free day. I was happily writing on the chalkboard when one of the newer students, Tamika, decided she wanted my chalk and demanded it. I ignored her until she found a piece of chalk to throw at me because I didn't comply. I let her know that, "If it hits me... I'm swingin'" and she made sure the next one made contact. So I threw a piece of chalk back and she charged at me and I fought for my life that day. It was so intense that her breasts popped out of her spaghetti strap shirt. The boys loved it but she quickly pulled them back in. By this time she was embarrassed and angry so she ran and grabbed a chair. I remember standing there frozen knowing that she was finally going to hurt me when the substitute snatched the chair out her hands. At the same time, the security guards were there to ensure our fight had concluded.

While I didn't wear makeup, I discussed the topic with my foster mother about how so many girls wore loads of it and she encouraged me to do the same. By this time she was worried about the possibility of me being gay and wanted to ensure that I wasn't. That became clear when a 19-year-old man was pursuing me at 13. I often attended the Boys and Girls Club on Saturdays and one day this older guy named Darren asked me if I wanted a soda. I told him "sure" and he bought me one. After that, Darren said nothing but began following me around the club. When I told my friends they said that was because he liked me and I should date him. I was so disgusted that I went home and told my foster mom and to my dismay, she agreed that I should date him. When I reminded her of his age, she let me know that again, she was OK with it.

I was so annoyed by her blessing that I decided to date him to spite her. So when I came to the club, my friends pushed us in an empty unlocked room to "get to know each other better." He stood in the opposite corner grinning. I stared for a few minutes and walked out, I couldn't do it. I felt I was too valuable to be putting my lips on just anybody.

My foster mother abandoned all rules when it came to me and boys. Everyone else couldn't talk to boys until about 16 and they couldn't even play with them but she made me! This boy flat out asked her if he could play with me and she said yes. There were days where he'd sit on my porch and stare at me as I was forced to be outside. There was this one time we played basketball briefly then he pinned me against the wall trying to touch me. I got away but never told my foster mother as I felt that she didn't care.

Those feelings of boys and men wanting to use my body and having no protection at home became more and more apparent. Sometimes, I'd stay after school and that meant I had to take the after-school bus home. Countless times I'd be pursued by older men and sometimes even followed. I'd run home and tell my foster mother about this and she'd reply, "They only wanted to rap to you." I wasn't going to be exploited in that way if I could help it.

Though seventh grade year was full of transitions and highs and lows, my foster mom gave me the best birthday party that year. I was turning 13. It started with a sleepover at her daughter's house. It was just me and my sisters (my sister and foster sisters) but we were able to be at our "big sister's house" which was Maria's middle child, Sherry, who was in her early 20's. We got to drink soda, eat chips and watch movies. She ensured we had a great time. Then that weekend she let me invite friends and she paid and reserved a skating party. The messed up part about it was that NONE of my "friends" came, but there were enough of us to have a good time and that we did. She really went all out that year, and I appreciated every moment of it.

By the time I was in eighth grade, my social life completely turned around. I had two best friends, Lakiesha Heard and Latoya Bertrand. Lilene was held back a year so we kind of lost touch. Alongside these two ladies were other friends whom I decided to start a group with called "AWJ," or Angels with Jesus. I told the girls that there was so much pressure to do the wrong things so we ought to make a vow to do the right things and hold each other accountable. We said we'd even ask our parents to allow us the freedom to hang out at the mall, etc… and we'd do positive things together.

However, AWJ started to dismantle quickly as several members started to date and become sexually active. It completely crumbled once this girl LaDonna and I were the only virgins left.

This is when I started to be extremely intentional. I created a list of things that I would and wouldn't do with a boy and also created a journal of how I wanted to parent my kids. Everywhere I went, I carried my parenting notebook and my sixth-grade yearbook. Those were two of my prized possessions. Imagine my hurt and pain when my guidance counselor called me into her office to let me know that someone had broken into my locker and poured all of the contents into a urinal. They couldn't salvage anything and they never found the culprit. I was so sad... Ms. Lee had wrote me a note and so did Ms. Bailey along with several of my peers that I'd revisit often and feel joy as I read them. That was taken away from me and to some it may appear as a random act and a small deal. However, for me, it was so much bigger than that. This act was strange because I didn't know anyone who had issues with me at that time and definitely knew about my secret possessions I kept in my locker. Furthermore, I'd continue to see sentimental, irreplaceable things destroyed. This is how I know now that those experiences transcended the physical and were spiritual. I believe that people unknowingly participated in destroying my history as I archived it. I didn't have baby pictures and there was no one to recreate a baby book and every time that I set to write or record my thoughts, there was someone to destroy portions of that EVERY TIME.

Though I continued with my principles of AWJ, I was eventually asked out by a boy named Kendall and I obliged. Kendall was a dark-skinned, skinny boy with a low 'fro. He was average height, very playful and full of life. Dating Kendall lasted about two weeks. I quickly learned that the expectations were too high. I was fine with sitting with him at the lunch table and me being entitled to his Hot Cheetos but at the end of the day, he wanted a hug. I played the run-and-chase game the first week but by the second week I took my time and wrote a note with the most verbose language I could muster. The language was so wordy and advanced that he wasn't sure what he was reading and he thought it was some sort of ode or love letter. It was my friends who I sent to then break the news to him when he came to them for consultation. They told him that I didn't like all of the affection and for that reason I was ending things. I remember the sadness that overtook Kendall's face and while I was sympathetic of his feelings, I was relieved to not have to dodge someone's touch everyday before I boarded the bus. While that hug seemed harmless, I knew I didn't like him like that, so to take a hug from him (affection has always been sacred to me...even then), I also knew of the possibility that hugging wouldn't be the end of it and eventually he'd want to kiss or more so I knew early on that I was in over my head and I needed to end it.

Other than the highs and lows of friendship, my eighth grade year was pretty fun! There was a new teacher who was originally from South Africa but was a white woman. She took a personal interest in me and my foster mother allowed her to take me to the movies once. We went to see Erin Brockovich. We had an OK time except she bought me the smallest box of popcorn and the movie wasn't very interesting to me. I had no say in the choice, and do not understand why a 14-year-old would find that interesting. I was, however, grateful for the gesture. There was a separate teacher who would sometimes call me into her room to do fun projects who was also a white woman. While I appreciated both of their efforts, the relationships didn't stick. These were different from the people I encountered prior who wanted to show me attention and care. I could feel the pity in their approach. There was always a prodding for information and not a genuine relationship that developed naturally. It was like they sought me out as their special "savior child". I had even asked the teacher who took me out to the movies if a friend could join us and she said, "No, she doesn't have it as hard as you. I want to just spend time with you." Looking back, I am not sure how they knew my situation besides reading paperwork that listed me as a foster child. I could've done without those engagements as they had no impact on my personal development. Mostly they felt uncomfortable yet I partook because they seemed so happy about it.

In many ways, I started to develop an identity and establish my values. My hair and clothes looked crazy but people didn't care as much. There really wasn't a popular crowd or no one who really had extremely nice clothes, so no one made that a thing at Kosciuszko.

One of the things I involved myself in was a program called "Teens Who Care". Teens Who Care was a program within my school that focused on service. We did things like clean up parks and tutor students at the school nearby. We also raised money for our school and with the teacher who oversaw it, we decided what we'd do with that money to enhance our school. School chorus was also amazing, and I choreographed the moves to our school song. That year meant that I would have the opportunity to take the eighth-grade choir trip (which was an overnight experience at a local hotel) and Teens Who Care also had an end-of-the-year trip. Finally, I was valedictorian so I looked forward to all of the year-end festivities.

The time would come when we were set to take the eighth grade trip. It started with a trip to Time Warner Cable. Ladonna and I were able to lead "When you Believe" by Mariah Carey and Whitney Houston while the rest of the choir backed us up! We thought we were celebrities as this would air on television.

From there, we had a two-day hotel trip planned. We were warned profusely about boys and girls not mixing, and the consequences of such. I wasn't stressing about that at all as I had no motivation to involve myself in those festivities. I was paired with one other girl but that girl was best friends with a different girl who also was great friends with another. Therefore they had their own hotel room but were always with us. That meant four girls would occupy my hotel room. One of those girls was Bonnie and while Bonnie was a sweet girl, she and Damian had a thing and that would land us in trouble.

Mid-year, our choir teacher got an assistant. Our choir teacher was a laid back middle-aged white man that we all adored. Though he should've cut all his hair off, he left the center balding and wore a small beard and maintained the hair that still clung to his head. He was so cool! He let us be creative and choir was always a great time of day! His assistant was a middle-aged black woman we all strongly disliked. She wore a short haircut that was gelled to her head most days, she was overweight and rocked oversized shirts and skirts. I am not sure if she was mean or if she felt she had to establish dominance because she came so late in the year, but she felt very mean and pretentious to us. We did not like her! We were told the rules with them, being that hotel doors stay open throughout the day while they were occupied (we had our own wing) and boys could hang in our rooms during the day time. Teachers were in constant flow and when it was "lights out," everyone had to go back to their rooms. The teachers stayed up extremely late to work this plan and got up extremely early to see it through.

That night, Bonnie missed Damion. All the girls including me (definitely peer pressure) decided that he could pay us a visit and no one would tell or object. It was a fun night. Damion showed us how to make his stomach ripple and we laughed and giggled all night. They slept in the bed together and we slept in pallets and the other bed respectively. Before we knew it, it was the morning and that meant room inspection. We were trapped! The teachers were posted outside our doors so we had no way to get Damion out. We were frantically trying to find a hiding spot for Damian! Should we hide him in the tub? No. Too easy, we thought!

We eventually decided that under the bed would work and it was just in time as we heard murmurings that Damion was missing and they knew Bonnie and Damion were an item. So here came "Ms. Meanie" the assistant teacher storming into our room on a man hunt. She looked around the room and went straight for the bathroom. What we'd learn, as we quickly hid Damion, was that we couldn't get under the bed as there were boards that went to the floor on all sides so we hid him at the foot of the bed on the floor and threw the comforter on top. He was instructed to lay still as a board.

Our plan worked and the assistant teacher/room inspector was headed out the door when she decided to be our mama as she liked to do. She snatched the comforter saying, "Have you no etiquette? Get this cover off the floor" and there was Damion! We were busted!

Because of our choice, the entire field trip was over. Every kid had to call home to make arrangements to be picked up. Our phone calls had to detail what we did while the teacher supervised to ensure we didn't leave any facts out.

I was so nervous as I never had any issues with boys or defying rules. My heart raced from the time I was caught until I got into the car. My foster mom asked me the details and didn't say much more. I asked her if I was in trouble and she said , "No... I know you had nothing to do with that boy." Though I was able to escape trouble at home, I received a three-day suspension from school. Upon arrival I had another meeting with our principal Mr. Valdez.

I never liked Mr. Valdez. I always felt that his consequences were extremely impersonal and mean. I imagine now that he probably wanted to maintain control and ensure compliance but he was out of touch. He wanted to meet with me separately to let me know that my actions weren't becoming of a valedictorian and a member of Teens Who Care. Therefore, he would take away my Teens Who Care trip as well. My heart was broken. How could I suffer an extra consequence especially when I was a bystander! No one else in that room was involved in the program, and I tried to explain that to him but he didn't budge. I also explained that he already suspended me and took away the rest of the hotel trip yet he was steadfast. I finally explained how I deserved this trip as I was faithful to the organization but he didn't care. It took me YEARS to get over that! I was in high school still mourning the loss of the Fun World field trip.

Eventually, that incident was in the past and it was time to "graduate" or complete 8th grade. As the valedictorian they decided they didn't want me to give a speech, so I gave opening remarks and introduced the principal. I entered my drawing for the eighth-grade graduation program and my design was also chosen for the back of the program. I wrote "2000" in box-square letters and had a few kids hanging from the numbers. At the top I wrote, "It's been great hanging around with you, but it's time to say our goodbyes." LaDonna and I wanted to do another duet of the Star-Spangled Banner to open our program but we were told that one of the teacher's daughter's (who was not a student) would do it as a token of appreciation for all of her contributions that year. We were livid and went back and forth about how it was unfair for a non-student to be given such an honor but they didn't care.

Back home, my foster mother made it clear that I wasn't getting a new dress, I was to find something in my closet. Then we went to her sister's house to borrow some tights as she said she couldn't find any in my size. To put things in perspective, in fifth grade I had a growth spurt. I shot up to 5-foot-5 and a size 10 shoe right before I got my first period. I remained thin but as middle school hit, I began to grow hips. My foster mother fought to conceal my hips. She let me know that now I had to wear big pants because my hip-to-waist ratio was too vast and I needed to wear big pants and shirts to conceal that. I am not sure why she worked so hard to conceal what I now know was a beautiful body but I suspect that it was envy. Her entire life she was picked on for being so thin and I think looking at me made her insecure. That same body would later be told I was "big" or "fat" and I believed every bit of it even with my flat stomach and small legs.

Her sister eventually found tights I could fit into. My foster mother had the financial means to buy me tights but I think she wanted to let me know that nothing was being bought. I'd learned many years later that her middle child had dropped out of high school a few years back and I think my ceremonies were cut short because she made sure I never outshone her biological daughters. All this awareness I acquired in adulthood through prayer. During those times, all I felt was unloved. It was about my inadequacy instead of the projection of inadequacy that others felt and imposed on me.

To make matters worse, my foster mother didn't even stay the entire graduation. She picked me up sometime after. When I asked her why, she said that menopause was making her periods extremely heavy and so she had to take care of herself. This could have been a real thing because she really was bleeding extremely heavily, or it could have been about the painful reality that her daughter, though she put her in the best suburban schools, didn't complete her schooling and that was a reminder. I am unsure.

I was still rocking a Jheri curl at that time and I was tired of how dry it was. She did do her due diligence to ensure I went to get it freshened up in the shop from time to time. However, right before my ninth-grade year, my foster mother and I had to stop getting my hair texturized and I was left to deal with my hair in its natural state. One day she bought me headbands with bows attached and said I should just rock a 'fro. This was before the natural-hair movement, and I thought that was grounds for constant bullying. I refused and cried and cried. Eventually to appease her I said I'd rock a 'fro and she said I didn't have to and she let me get some braids. By the end of the summer of my eighth grade year, I decided to press my hair myself. I knew that it was possible for it to fall out as there was still texturizer in it but I didn't care. It didn't fall out and that was my physical declaration that the wave nouveau was no more.

The end of eighth grade also meant the end of playing with dolls which I had to give up at 14. I was obsessed with my dolls. Their names were Emily, Emilia (Emily's sister after she died... and looked very much like her. She was thrown away because she got thrown around by boys in the neighborhood and was too dirty to clean up), Michelle and Beatrice. On the weekends and in the summer, they were dressed and hair was combed every day. I bought them bows and barrettes. I talked to them and they came to life in my dreams. On their birthday (the anniversary of the day I received them), I gave them a small bite of cake (from a $0.25 cake I bought from the corner store) and though it was still there later, I swore they ate a small piece, just small enough that I couldn't see. I read to them and slept with them.

I'm not sure how long I would've continued to play with dolls, but it abruptly came to an end when one day I tried to take one of my babies on a grocery store run with myself and my foster mom. She matter-of-factly said to me, "Girl, it's time to stop playing with dolls before someone thinks you're retarded." And as harsh as that sounded, I knew she was right but I couldn't dare get rid of my humans who I convinced myself were real and only pretended to not have souls and a mind, so I gave them to Stacy's foster kids she had at that time so that they could be adopted and live a full life.

Before giving them away, I told them about them being real and how they must take care of them. I told them that I didn't just snatch them up or throw them on the floor and if you drop them, you apologize, because you wouldn't want them to turn on you in your sleep. Her foster daughter's Kokesha and Danielle were eager and absorbed every word. They couldn't wait to be a mommy to my babies.

So imagine my horror, shock and dismay when I went over Stacy's house to hang out (as she sometimes took us to her house to hang with us as our big sister) and checked on my babies and she told me she threw them away. When I asked her why she said they woke up crying saying they heard the dolls talking. I was devastated but I couldn't reveal that it was me who gave them that idea. I simply prayed to God that they died peacefully and let it go.

Ch.6

PASSAGE TO TRANSFORMATION

Before I knew it, it was time for high school which was the first time in my life I was able to make a major decision. I was really interested in Milwaukee High School of the Arts. I wanted to sing and dance and my foster mother had strictly forbade it, often saying, "Not now... I'll let you do it later." However, later never came and this was my opportunity. Milwaukee High School of the Arts also wanted me. A recruiter had originally met me when they came to Kosciuszko and once they found out I was a straight-A student interested in the arts, they were vying for me, too. The problem was my foster mother wanted me to go to Messmer. I was accepted into the Choice Program and offered a full-ride scholarship if School Choice ever failed and she felt that Milwaukee High School of the Arts wasn't academically sound enough. I ended up having a conversation with my social worker and telling her the conundrum and she informed us both that it was my decision. My foster mother was so angry about her loss of power/believing this was the best choice for me and I was so sad to disappoint her that I relented and went to Messmer.

At this time in my life my former 5th grade teacher and I had reconnected and she became a major support in my life. It started off with us sending journals back and forth when my sister would have her two years later and I was in middle school going to visit her after I'd walked home from high school (I'd pass my elementary school on the way home).

During this time, Mrs. Evans was in her mid-thirties and married with three children. She was a thin woman with a medium-brown complexion. She loved to wear her hair curled (bumped) up or under. She loved a red lip and taught in high heels most days. She was overall stunningly beautiful.

Mrs. Evans was doing her best to be available when I needed her. I was attending church frequently and I had a school where people supported me as well. I made sure I stayed in activities to limit the time I would be at home.

Messmer started off really rocky but eventually I'd see that it was all in God's plan. I had spent most of my time in middle school on the southside and all my friends chose schools on the southside since that is where they lived. So I ended up going to a high school where I hardly knew anybody except a few faces from elementary school. There was this one girl in particular whose name was Latoya. I knew Latoya from elementary school. In fact, our then-teacher Mrs. Evans once had a movie day and said that we could bring blankets and stuffed animals. I opted to bring my new doll. Latoya asked to play with her and I never saw her again! There were times I'd ask about my baby who I never even got to name but she always said she'd bring her tomorrow and tomorrow turned to never. I couldn't tell my foster mom about it as she would know I gave away something of mine I wasn't supposed to bring out the house so eventually I just chalked it up as a loss and stopped asking.

Therefore, it goes without saying that Latoya knew exactly who I was. Latoya in elementary was nothing special. She always had short hair that her mom kept in neat ponytails. She was thin with dark-brown skin. There was even a time when Latoya tried to bully a girl named Marcy after we finished lining up from using the restroom and Marcy beat her up with the side of her fists and politely walked in class after. Latoya was distraught and speechless but wanted to come to high school like she was macho.

One day early in the school year, Latoya saw me and asked me what my name was. When I told her, she pretended to recall where she knew me from until she figured out it was the elementary school we went to five blocks away from our high school. After that she decided to recruit some friends and begin to bully me. For the most part I ignored it but I did go home and tell my foster mom. She told me I needed to talk to the administration at the school. Messmer was different. With it being a private school, they were governed by different rules. They had a zero-tolerance policy against fighting and so fighting my bully wasn't an option if I wanted to maintain my status as a student at Messmer High School.

When I reached out, they sent me to Ms. King and from that day, my life was changed. Ms. King was (and still is) the most beautiful woman on the planet. Her beauty is striking and undeniable. It is hard to believe that she stands about 5-foot-1 and has a tiny frame because when she's dealing with you, you forget how small she really is and her hugs engulf you even though her arms are tiny.

I came to her office broken and in search of relief. I was hoping that it wouldn't be the same as it was in middle school where nothing ever really got resolved. Ms. King brought Latoya into her office and gave us both an opportunity to speak. Once she got to the bottom of it, she'd check the bully and comfort the victim and everything would be good in the world. You'd both also leave with a hug in the end as well. After that moment, I lived for her energy. If someone looked at me sideways, they were in the office 'cause I was telling. For the first time in my life I felt protected, seen and loved. Now, there were times my foster mother Maria certainly protected me but the combination of being protected, seen and loved at once felt new. Honestly, getting bullied was fun for a while because it meant that I'd get time with Ms. King.

The newness of that wore off quickly though but the bullying did not stop. One time I was drinking a glass of water and an upperclassman stopped me and said, "Hey, he likes you," and pointed to a random boy only for that random boy to yell, "No I don't!" and the hallways erupted with laughter.

However there was this one time I was over tattling. We were in the hallway and one of my classmates came up to me telling me that she heard I was talking about her. This girl, her entourage as and I knew that this wasn't true! I barely talked in school at all but I guess they wanted the entertainment and I was an easy target. She came up to me and said, "Jamie said that you've been talking about me behind my back."

I replied, "No I haven't."

She wasn't satisfied with my response so she responded, "Well, I just wanted you to know that if you were, I'll beat your ass so you betta keep my name out your mouth!"

Her threats were so played out and yawn worthy that I very calmly said, "Are you done?" and when she had nothing but a stunned look on her face, I walked away... BIG mistake. That day I learned to never turn your back on an enemy.

At this phase in life, I used to buy braiding hair, gel my hair into a ponytail then wrap the braiding hair around my ponytail into a huge bun. I got maybe four steps away when my phony pony was used to throw me to the ground. I was caught off-guard and while I fought back, I lost that fight. I was knocked to the ground. A lot of the fight I completely blacked out. I remember almost gaining the strength to push myself off the ground and being knocked down again, I remember getting my face stomped in and some of the other students eventually pulling her off of me.

This was the day I met Ms. Childs, our assistant principal. Ms. Childs was a tall, medium-brown-skinned woman who always wore a smile no matter what. She always wore her hair straight down. It was thick and fell below her shoulders and it was always neatly trimmed. Here I was with my hair all over my head, my phony pony in the garbage can... looking rough. I can only imagine her initial thoughts meeting me in this way for the first time. She interviewed us both before our suspensions. I told her what happened before the fight but when I couldn't recall most of the details of what happened. She had a look of skepticism. We would both be eventually suspended so that that gave time for things to cool down (Messmer only averaged about three fights a year) and to make a determination of who was expelled because fighting was an automatic grounds for expulsion. By the grace of God and them interviewing some of the other students who witnessed it, it was determined that I was dragged into the fight (literally) and could do nothing but attempt to defend myself (which I did horribly).

Two things that I heard constantly from my foster mother was that I was fat and gay. These two things couldn't be further from the truth but as a child growing into herself and depending on the adults in my life to affirm me, I fought hard not to believe them. The name calling became a struggle for me. Something in me told me that in order to not make the names stick, I had to tell myself 10 times that I wasn't whatever name I was called. So I'd recite " I'm not gay...I'm not gay... I'm not gay," like a monk reciting his chants. While that helped temporarily I definitely had conversations in my alone time with God pleading with Him to not be gay. I even remember creating a pretend relationship in my head with pop star Aaron Carter in order to ensure I wasn't gay. I did my best to turn the hormones on, but to no avail. I had no interest in boys in those days.

High school was the time I developed a deeper relationship with Mrs. Evans and my bond with Ms. King was just budding. Sometimes my foster mom would read my diary where I expressed how much I loved Ms. King and Mrs. Evans and called me gay. In addition to that she'd say I wanted to take Mrs. Evans from her husband. It wasn't like that at all, and I think she knew that. Did I sometimes fantasize what it would be like if they were my mother? Absolutely, but that was the extent of that.

In order to cope with the lack of affection in our home, I asked God to give me an alternative life. I asked God if I could have dreams where I had a mother and a father who loved me. It took awhile but eventually the dreams started to manifest. In my dreams I was about 3 years old and my name was Kari and I would go on adventures with my dream mother and father. If I was sick, they comforted me... if I was scared, they protected me. I was the only child and everything to them. Every night I prayed to have those dreams but they'd only come randomly but when I awoke, I felt happy and at peace and hopeful that I'd have my dream parents when I needed them.

During this same time, I started attending this church with one of my foster mother's family members and met this lady named Gerry. Gerry was a beautiful brown-skinned, tall, slender woman who had a gentle spirit. She always showed me kindness and what appeared to be individual attention. In my quest to have more of that type of love, I wrote her a note asking her to be my godmother. Imagine my heartbreak when she wrote me back saying, "No, sorry, I can't."

Notes, journaling and expressing myself with words was always my thing. I was always an artistic child. There wasn't much support in my home but it didn't stop me. I wrote my first poem randomly in the fourth grade called "Proud Beauty" and it never stopped from there. When I was in high school, I entered a poetry contest that the library sponsored and won third place in the first round. I walked to the library alone and performed with no support even though my foster mom was well aware of what I was doing. The next round took place downtown so I needed a ride. I convinced my foster mom to take me by telling her that there was a cash prize and the judges giving me good feedback my first time around. I did not place the second time and when I came home I was basically told that there was no surprise that I didn't advance as she figured I wouldn't, but I insisted so she gave in.

Most of my events were like that. I loved to perform so I'd enter talent shows etc. and do it all alone. It hurt my feelings, but I wanted to do what I loved more than seeing people I cared about support me. Though I didn't understand that then, lack of support became a mantra or one of life's motifs. The truth is I felt empty, unimportant and unloved but my drive is God-given! Nobody could stop me because God continued to push me!

Along those same lines of creativity, I journaled or recorded myself on cassette tape. This was where I placed my dreams, my fears, and my hopes. My tapes were my therapy. I would stay up late at night and either go inside the bathroom or closet and have some amazing sessions. To this day, my closet and bathroom are sources of comfort and signify peace for me and to this day I record myself and journal in both places!

Around the age of 16, I started to experience what some would call sleep paralysis but I identify it as demons. It was much more than being locked down to the bed. The first time it happened, I recall sleeping with my back toward the wall. The day had already broke and I was working to get as much sleep as possible when I felt a strong force that disabled me from shifting to the other side. Earlier that night I felt a presence in my bed, but I assumed it was my sister who would sometimes get scared at night and get in my bed. As I came fully awake, I tried to turn and realized I couldn't move. That is when it happened. As my back faced the door a dark figure came up behind me and placed its arm in front of my face. Its arm was black but translucent. It said, "Are you gonna save us?" At this time, I began to panic and pray but in my mind. I couldn't speak or scream from my mouth. When I finally came to, I began to blurt at the air, "Save you from what... I can't save you ! Only Jesus can!" But whatever was there was gone.

I had been through many therapists in my tenure at Maria's house. When I was younger it was a joke. No one was really trying to get to the heart of my issues. It was clear that they were making money off of me and cared nothing about my mental health. I could tell that many were racists and that annoyed me even more.

There was one session I had with a therapist named Harry. Even though I was molested by a woman, men made me uncomfortable. However, I realize through preparing to write this book that there is more to me left to uncover. As I was preparing to write this book, I spoke to one of my older brothers to compare his early memories with mine. During this conversation, he revealed that a male family member molested several of us. I stopped short of asking if I was a victim as I was not ready to deal with the realities of that but as I see my fear continue to play out in my life, I know it's a conversation I have to have.

At any rate, I was extremely uncomfortable with men who sat with their legs all the way open and sat facing me. This was Harry. Not only that, but he only had one question, "Tell me what your brothers did." This baffled me because I had recently spoken to my foster mother about one incident with one of my brothers, but Harry had some impression that there was some massive molestation going on. I was not comfortable sharing that experience with him and I felt like he would be looking for more than that incident which I didn't have for him.

Our sessions were always the same. He would play a board game with me and when he grew tired of playing he'd say, "Now let's talk about your brothers." with his stank gapped legs open. In my mind I'm like if you don't get your excited self somewhere! I'll never forget this older gentleman with his box-cut 'fro and salt-and-pepper beard. Ugh, he irked me.! I didn't spend many sessions with Harry and when they switched me to another psychiatrist, I asked what happened to Harry and they said, "He's no longer with us." I made some assumptions as to why. I felt and still feel that he did not have the right mindset to be practicing there and Lord only knows what happened with a client who wasn't as rebellious as I.

That incident in question was a strange event that I think had less to do with sexuality and more with naughty boys. My brother loved to mess with me. My sister was the oldest and then my mom had four boys before she had me. I think they were excited to have a little sister to tortue because they did many mean things to me. One thing was when they sang me this song, "Open your mouth, close your eyes and you will find a big surprise." I followed the directions of the jingle and one of my brothers proceeded to pee in my mouth. When I got wind of it I spit it out ! They never tried to make me suck their penises or anything, so I did not understand what story Harry wanted. So while the incident was grotesque, it wasn't what Harry was looking for.

A therapy adventure honorable mention goes to when I "graduated" from therapy in about the fifth grade. I am not sure how one does that because I hadn't received any healing. The therapist took me across the hospital to a bakery and stared at me as I ate a cupcake. It was the strangest and fakest exchange. I hated the look of pity with a smile...where you can see that someone thinks less of you but they're so proud of themselves for treating you with some dignity.

I would return to therapy in high school. It was still a joke and a ploy. I started off back at the same facility where I "graduated" where I received "group therapy". This therapy was with other teenagers and to my surprise and embarrassment, one of my classmates was also in these sessions. None of us wanted to be there and so much of our healing was supposed to come from what our parents or foster parents said we needed to work on. One time, this girl's grandmother came to the session when her granddaughter whom she had custody over wouldn't discuss her issues as they always pushed for us to do. She interrupted her silence and uttered, "Tell them. Tell them about the dirty socks under your bed and the bloody sanitary napkins you didn't throw away." That made her clam up even more, and I am sure that was illegal for them to do but intentional. There was a locked door you must pass through to get to the therapist offices and another door that was locked that housed the session. She was invited in and I'm sure that only stunted her therapeutic healing. As a whole, we made no progress. We all had attitudes and a white lady named Naomi with a sing-song voice led these sessions pretending to be empathetic when I know in her head she was saying "these niggas" wasn't about to heal me!

So therapy became the way to put me on and keep me on depression pills. I found a way to pretend to take them and spit them out on the way to school. I was very aware that my issues were circumstantial and not internal. One time during my refill consultation, I got bold instead of remaining silent and letting my foster mother describe these exaggerated things about me. She'd say things like, "She isolates herself... she doesn't want to hang with the other kids in the home," which I'd normally say nothing out of fear/respect of what would happen if I spoke against anything she said.

But that day I interjected saying, "I do hang with my siblings. We create dances and sing and all of that."

Her reply was, "Girl ain't nobody talkin' about those monkey dances you sometimes make them do."

At that point I shut up because I had just touched the shore of "disrespect" and didn't want to cross into that river. I had seen what can happen if you go all the way to the edge.

About a year before this conversation, I was given a job by one of the lead staff members at the Boys and Girls Club, Carla Jackson. Carla was a woman who saw everyone's potential. She was in her 30s, an avid Packers and Michael Jackson fan with short hair and an ever-caring demeanor. At that time she created the most fun programming at the Boys and Girls Club. Initially the job was going well but sometimes the kids were disrespectful. Maria would pick me up every day and she made me pay for gas for this exchange. I was already irritated at that because I made about $150 every two weeks and she made me give her gas money in order to be picked up yet I'd seen her pick up her daughter who was in her 20s with no charge and help her pay her bills! Yet I kept that to myself. I got in the van after my shift and she asked me how my day went. I told her how I got into it with one of the kids because their mouth was slick and she told me, "You gotta learn to be quiet before you don't have a job." Etiquette according to Maria would dictate that at that point you close your mouth but I didn't. I said, "I get that and most times I do but sometimes I can't help it." Well she didn't like that rebuttal and so she came back at me with, "You gotta learn to shut up … that's why people don't like you now." By this point in the game, I had learned to combat her negative talk. Maria wasn't really someone who physically abused you (she did have a mean pinch where she'd pinch you and turn it and grab you in multiple places in that pattern) but boy, she emotionally abused you! What I'd typically do when I was called , fat, gay, bitch, etc. was go in my closet and call her out her name.

The exchange would go something like this:

Maria: " Bitch...If it had've been a sandwich you would've found it."

Me in my closet: "You a bitch. Bitch" (smile). Then I'd go in my closet and tell myself 10 times that I wasn't a bitch before I started to let the words penetrate. The Holy Spirit gave me the insight to pump myself up after being called a name … the cussing back in secret was all me.

So with me being in the car I had to say something before I believed the hurtful things she said, I turned to her and said, "People do like me," and that's when she slapped me. Followed by her saying, "Like I said, nobody likes you! Ms. King is doing her job and Mrs. Evans is being nice! You think you're gonna take Mrs. Evans from her husband but you're not. And if you say something else slick, you can find your own way home!"

So I sat there in silence with my heart turning cold toward her.

So I knew once she had her rebuttal to my rebuttal in that psychiatrist's office, I knew to shut up. However, that really hurt my feelings. Maria's punishments were to make you feel like you did not matter at all. She'd make you go in your room, give all the kids money to go to the store, make sure they parade past you with their goodies and no one could talk to you at all. Or everyone got an invite to her oldest daughter's house except me or got to go out with her while I was left alone. She did a lot of divide-and-conquer so it was hard to have true relationships among the siblings. At any time, we were her pawns and because we were constantly fighting for any type of love and attention, anytime we got it ...even if it was fake, we rolled with it. If we were the favorite or "not in trouble" then we certainly ostracized whoever was, as instructed.

After that, we got my pills and no follow-up questions were asked. He made money by how many kids he medicated and foster children were the easiest to do this to. My foster mother received more money having a psychiatric label attached to my name as that meant I was more difficult to deal with so they had to pay her more to keep/support me (that isn't necessarily her doing but how the system works).

I would only go to that facility a little while longer before she'd transfer me to a new facility where I'd get one-on-one sessions. This was an older African American woman and I had had it with these handpicked psychologists/ psychiatrists who believed everything my foster mother said. The first time I met Ms. Williams, she had a chip on her shoulder. It was if she wanted to be bourgeois but she was ghetto in real life. She looked to be about mid 50s or early 60s. She had brown skin, a short wig and large cankles. She was not a beautiful woman. She thought being bourgeois was exaggerating annunciations when you speak (the type of annunciation that people associate with "talking white") and looking down her nose at people.

By this time I could read people and I had a mouth on me when I wasn't home. She couldn't slap me or call me names so I was going to use this opportunity as my therapy but not in the way that they thought.

Ms. Williams would ask me questions and I'd be short with her. She'd sit at her desk that was about 12 feet away from the couch she had me sit on and discuss whatever my foster mother said I did. "Why did you put salt in the sugar?... Why did you break the dryer? You can tell me , I have to keep what you say private." Yet when I told her that those weren't my doings, she didn't want to accept that. She believed my foster mom because according to her I also was a compulsive liar. So she continued to pry and annoy me.

One day in predictable bourgeoisie fashion, she told me how she had a client, an African American boy who was in need of new shoes. She said if she saw him again with raggedy shoes, she was going across the street to the mall to buy him some.

I pressed her by saying, "So you let him wear those raggedy shows how many times? And now you want to get him some? Yours are leaning so I hope you get you some too."

Ms. Williams couldn't lose her job or blow her cover so she told me how it was clear I was angry and she was a big girl and she could take it.

When she wasn't speaking nonsense, she was asleep! I don't know if she had epilepsy or she was clocking a massive amount of billing hours but our sessions were around 6 p.m. and she went to sleep on me on several occasions. I would share this experience with my younger sister who came to have sessions with her too and she reported the same thing! I never woke her up until it was time to go, I was happy not to have to play this game of "Why did you do this?" Not to mention she told our foster mother everything we said. If I knew then what I know now, I would have sued her.

One of the positive things that came out of these therapy sessions happened very randomly. My two best friends at the time, Charisma and Riley, came to therapy with me because we were going to the mall after. Ms. Williams was even rude to them. She told them, "Make sure you straighten those magazines back up when you're done," before they barely touched one and then interrupted our session to tell them they were too loud when they barely chuckled out loud in the waiting room.

So I survived another session and we were inside the office building waiting for the bus. I started singing to myself and as this man walked in he stopped and said, "Who was that singing?" I told him that I was singing and he told me how he had a studio in the building and he'd love to work with me.

Call it naivete but I always wanted to sing so we went to his studio. I told him that my friends could also sing and so he told us that we should come up with a name for ourselves and start to write some music. Once we had music, he'd start to record us.

I took this task very seriously and after throwing names out I came up with the name Triversity. I felt that this name fit us because we were three girls but very different in many ways. The first song I wrote for us was called "Take Me Away."

The chorus of the song went:
"Take me away
Lead me on,
To a place where
We can go strong
To an ocean or a hill
It doesn't matter ...I'll love you still

Dream me a dream
Write me a song
Give me a reason
To carry on
Give me hope
Give me a vision
Let me know,
It's not (just) intuition"

As soon as we had practiced the lyrics, we went into the studio and recorded. Immediately I noticed that Riley wasn't serious and Charisma was very shy. After we finished recording, he set us up with a woman who provided us with voice lessons for free.

I was very excited and did everything I could to write and attend the voice lessons. However after about two months, Riley told me she didn't want to sing and Charisma said she wanted to pursue modeling instead. I was so mad at them and felt that out of respect for Jefferey who gave us this opportunity and paid for our voice lessons, I'd have to let him know they didn't want to do it so we'd have to pass. He was really disappointed. He wanted me to move away from love songs and write gospel music. He really wanted us to become gospel recording artists and I let my friends take that opportunity from me.

While battling growing up, school work, friendships and relationships, Maria and I continued to bump heads, we could not get beyond always being in cahoots with each other. I used to get up early in the morning and rehearse how we'd make it work. In my head I'd plan each day saying to myself, "OK, I am going to come home... clean my room and watch the kids. I'll then ask her if she needs help with anything." It didn't work. I'd get accused of things I didn't do under the pretense she thought I was mad at her or it looked like something I would do. I couldn't defend myself or present evidence to clear my name as that was considered talking back and disrespectful.

Things became so toxic that she required that my part-time job be what I used to buy school supplies and clothes. I was livid as I barely made any money. Adding to that issue I needed an expensive calculator I couldn't afford and she reminded me that that was my responsibility. That caused my grades to slip.

I was so mentally exhausted from fighting so hard to be perfect, I stormed into Ms. King's office during this time and before she could ask what was wrong I began to scream, "I hate her... I hate her...I hate her". She just hugged me so tight and we talked about why I felt that way and she settled me enough to be able to return to class with a mind that was clear to focus. There would be many days where I felt like I was losing my sanity and Ms. King would remind me that there was hope. At the end of it all, she'd always be like, "Now go wipe your face ... and return to class." It was her basically saying "Alright, go fight another fight but don't show anyone you just came out of war." I don't know how people in these circumstances make it out without their "Ms.King" but God definitely planned this union and the sun has been brighter in my life ever since and I pray He never takes her from me.

The time came where progress reports came in the mail and I had a "D" in math. Normally I'd freak out as I worked hard to be an honor student but I had a callus around my emotions. She came into the room where I had just volunteered to do my foster sister Myonda's hair and started screaming at me about my grades. I was so annoyed that I decided to talk under my breath knowing that it would lead to destruction.

After yelling at me, she walked out of the room and continued to fuss. I started mumbling, "Oh so now you care... I been told you I needed a calculator and now you mad? Oooooo Kaaaay."

I saw Katrice's eyebrows go up because she was ready to start some drama but I didn't care, I put the bait out there. Katrice left the room to tell Maria what I said.

Maria came back and asked me if I said those things and with a smirk I said, "No" just to annoy her. At that point she began to hit me. I felt nothing. I saw images like the time she stood on my feet when her pinches didn't hurt and tried to hurt me by putting her full weight on my feet...and the time her daughter threatened my life because "I was talking slick to her mama" or the time her daughter blamed me then a 13-year-old for causing a rift in her and her mom's relationship but I had transcended this pain! I was over it!

After a few hits, I yelled, "Don't touch me, I'm not your child." She froze in place. She didn't recognize me anymore, and she kicked me out that day.

I had just come home. She allowed me to stay with Mrs. Evans' sister that weekend (something she didn't normally do) and I believe she did it to save face and it actually irritated her. Maria had an issue with us forming bonds with people so I knew she wouldn't be glad to see me. That is why I came in ready to do acts of service to smooth things over. I took the bag I had already had packed from the weekend and walked out as she ordered.

As I was walking trying to figure out my next move I remembered how I had a chat with her boyfriend who was the father to her children and a father figure to us, too. He was driving through the neighborhood one day and my friend Charisma and I were walking to the store. He gestured for us to come inside the car. Once inside he had Charisma introduce herself and he told her that she must be going through things at home because friends who are close share similar stories or they'd lack compatibility. Then with tears in his eyes he said, "She's jealous of you and I'm tired of it. I usually stay in my place and not say anything because I am not a foster parent but I'm sick of it... and she keeps threatening to kick you out.

Well guess what, you're not going anywhere! If she ever tries to really put you out again, that's when I'm putting my foot down." I thanked him, he gave us some money and I told him I'd see him later on at the house.

Unfortunately he wasn't home when this all went down but I appreciated his words more than he'll ever know. There weren't many times I was offered protection growing up or even the notion of being seen so I appreciated it because I knew he meant every word.

Ch.7

GALUMPH TO GLORIA'S

When I was kicked out, I remembered Maria's words, "You think the grass is greener on the other side but it ain't." But I was optimistic. I hoped for a young mother filled with love like I imagined Ms. King or Mrs. Evans would be if I were their child. Yet upon seeing Gloria, that hope died. She looked like the black version of the witch in Hansel and Gretel and she turned out to act just like she looked.

In her defense, I never gave her a chance. I went right into the room she said was mine to sulk. I closed those doors quickly and that's where I stayed unless I had to use the restroom. It wasn't too long until she was ready to show me off to her friends. I didn't come out, but I did peek through the blinds in the door.

I came to live with Gloria the summer before my sophomore year and that was the year my high school changed its uniform policy. We went from being able to wear whatever we wanted to being required to wear collared shirts. They were trying to break up the dichotomy of the haves and the have-nots.

Gloria often bragged about her daughter's house she "got built from the ground" and how we were going to visit. She told me that that would be when we got my school clothes. She also asked me where I got my clothes from and when I told her places like Kohls and the JCPenny she said, "Good, because I don't buy cheap clothes." One thing about Maria is she did clothe and feed us so I was being honest when telling Gloria that many of my clothes came from those stores.

While I had no intention to bond with Gloria, I was excited to see this house she bragged about...until it was time to go. I started to feel major anxiety before the trip and I did not want to go but I had no choice because I had nowhere else to go. I did not like the idea of being in a completely foreign environment. To this day I feel like that. Even when I go on vacations and enjoy myself, after a while I want to go home. Being in spaces that aren't mine makes me feel like I felt moving to another foster home so while I know I am not having that experience, my emotional cortex is having that experience and I am not sure how to completely subdue that yet.

Gloria and her friend did the driving. As we started the road trip, I was so disturbed with her spending! She took so much money out of the bank and gave her friend a ton of it for driving. I really didn't understand why she was being so flashy and loose with her money until I realized that she was showing off and it must've been her first check for me!

Her daughter's house was beautiful and she did exchange a hello with me but we didn't even stay long. Her mission was to go shopping. I was actually looking forward to this part as she had told me that she didn't buy cheap clothes and I saw how much money she had. She went into a store and purchased several things for herself. She informed me that she'd purchase my collared shirts back in Milwaukee but she'd get my jeans while we were here. She went into the Levi's store and bought me two pairs of jeans. I was so disturbed and disappointed. I couldn't fathom how she thought two pairs of pants was enough for me to start school with! When we did get back to Wisconsin, she bought me five of the ugliest button-up collared shirts from Walmart (yes the lady who didn't buy cheap clothes).

Back in her home, I enjoyed my room pitch black and away from the noise until the demons started to bother me! The first time was the creepiest thing I had ever seen and it was as if out of a movie. I had a teddy bear sitting on the nightstand. One night, the bear levitated and started to float toward me. The bear floated and stopped right in front of my face! Once again I was frozen in place and unable to speak. When I was freed, I turned on all the lights and sat up in shock, completely still.

Gloria was a church-going woman and had always said I could tell her anything. This time I was so traumatized I had to give it a try. I told Gloria what I experienced and she decided that her "stanky preacher friend" as she called her behind her back would come over and pray for me and her house. This time I came out to partake in the process because I was terrified. Her friend went through the house and prayed for the house as well as for me. I was done with that room for a while and resorted to sleeping on the couch.

It wasn't long until I was introduced to her granddaughter who lived three houses down and was around the same age as me. One day she told her grandmother about her best friend-Charlene who was a foster child who needed a home and before I knew it, her best friend was living with us. Charlene and I never had any issues nor did her granddaughter and I, we just didn't click. They were actually smitten with each other and I was such an outsider. I soon learned why. They were heavily into boys and sexual activity and they enjoyed exchanging stories.

Gloria also took to Charlene. They were a great pair. Charlene was able to receive an allowance and nice clothes. First, Gloria said it was because Charlene didn't have much but later it became apparent that it was because she actually liked her. Charlene was more personable than I, and she was pretty. Charlene may have been treated well for a number of reasons and it could be mostly because she naturally bonded with Gloria or Gloria felt like she saw herself in her, but Charlene was light-skinned with long hair and some black people get awestruck about things like that. I never really took the time to explore why there was a stark difference between the way we were treated, but it was distinctive!

I soon came to find out through her interactions with Charlene that Gloria hid snacks. Initially Charlene was telling me all the chips and soda were hers and that her uncle purchased her those items and she asked Gloria to keep them. I would later find out that Gloria hid her snacks and she allowed Charlene access to them. The demons didn't stop, either. Eventually Gloria kicked me off the couch and I was fine because Charlene was there now and we shared a room but her presence changed nothing. One day when we were waking up for school, I saw a piece of string land and fall on my face. It divided my face in half. I couldn't move or speak but I could hear Charlene and Gloria's granddaughter in the background. After fighting to unfreeze and finally being released I sat up to half of my face in pain. It was exactly where the string divided my face! Before I could make any sense of what had just happened Charlene blurted out, "What's wrong with you?" I knew I couldn't trust her so I pretended to have no idea what she was referring to. It did give me some reassurance to know that what I was experiencing was indeed real. We never discussed what she saw but she indeed saw me endure that spiritual battle with her naked eye and she looked horrified!

Gloria wasn't having too much of that demon talk. Before I knew it she was requesting that I take depression pills. At first I wasn't going for it until I realized that I did not care to fight. I started to take those pills and they indeed made me feel depressed. I was moving in the world like a zombie when I'd take those pills and never had motivation to do anything.

These pills changed me completely. It was as if my physical body and my spirit were separate. I had every motivation in my mind/spirit to be myself...to dance/sing when I wasn't in the drama that was my life but I couldn't. I was so weak...the pills made me depressed.

School was my solace but my battleground as well. Kids started to notice that I had three pairs of pants that I changed up each week and the talking started. I just took most of it in stride and did my best to ignore it. That worked out until one day my classmate Melody was being a little too playful ribbing me. In her defense it was all in jest but I was at a boiling point at that moment. Quiet Dianne flipped out on Melody, and we ended up in the hallway with the teacher for conflict resolution. I remember standing up and daring her to fight right before the hallway intervention. Now I went to a Catholic school and one fight would've led to an expulsion but I did not care at that time. I am so appreciative that Melody was so shocked and didn't want to fight. While in the hallway she apologized, and I calmed down and realized that I was taking everything out on her.

School was never that bad because Ms. King was there. There was this one time I got extremely sick and to this day I don't know what was wrong with me. I went to Ms. King's office and she immediately knew I wasn't feeling well. Anytime I was sick in Maria's house I was sent to my room to sleep. I'd be checked on throughout the day but that would be it. Ms. King had me go see the nurse. He took my temperature and asked me if I had been tested for diabetes. I told him no but he told me that I needed to drink juice. I can't remember if he sent me home but I didn't go home. I went to Ms. King's office after he gave me juice. She sent me to the computer lab that was attached to the office and let me sleep. That is another day I won't forget because that was the first time I felt like someone cared about my well-being. Ms. King showed me so much concern and love that day that I kind of understood why kids enjoyed being sick. I know she doesn't know it, but she taught me how love was supposed to feel and what love was supposed to look like and I am grateful for that. Her love made love an action word. I learned how love felt and looked like through her.

Ms. King wasn't the only kind person during this time. Gloria had a son who was nothing like her. One day he invited me to his house as he said that he knew I was bored. I was very terrified as I was afraid of men and felt that most wanted to take advantage of me. But I took a chance and he was extremely nice. When we got to his house, he cooked me a delicious meal and gave me the remote and the television. He talked with me a little and let me relax.

I was sincerely appreciative of his kindness. He knew his mom and I didn't have the best relationship but he chose to be kind to me on his own. Even her daughter who lived three doors down didn't want anything to do with me.

Gloria and I never found our rhythm, and my older sister who I talked to regularly at that time got tired of me complaining and suggested that I go live with my "Aunt Trisha" and promised that the grass was greener on the other side.

Ch.8

TREK TO TRISHA'S

I am usually a good judge of character but Trisha fooled me for a very short time. I remember how the idea to stay with Trisha came about. At this time I was in constant conversation with my older sister Alberta (Tinkie). One day she said to me, "You should stay with Trisha. If you do, you'll have money in your pocket and your head (hair) will stay done."

In my soul I knew it wasn't a good idea, but my heart wanted to give it a try. When I arrived I was so eager. After unpacking, I sat on the side of her bed in a chair and told her so many things. I don't remember what I shared besides the fact that I was talking so long that she fell asleep. That's when I noticed a roach walking across the floor carrying a strand of spaghetti. I didn't know it then but the roach was foreshadowing of what was to come: a low-down, dirty shame of an adventure.

I can't remember when things started to go bad. Initially, she braided my hair and things were looking fine. I shared a room with Trisha's young sons. There was a bunk bed and a single bed and my bed was whichever one that they chose not to sleep on that particular night. They were about 3 and 6 years old at the time.

At this time in my life, I began to fall in love with my shape. I had a flat stomach, hips and overall nice curves. For everything I said about myself Trisha had a rebuttal. I'd say, "My stomach is so flat," she'd say, "Is it all the way flat? Let me see it." Because Ms. King was becoming increasingly significant in my life, anyone who knew me would hear an earful about Ms. King. Just imagine my surprise when one day I was called into the office and there was Trisha in some overalls and her best professional voice in Ms. King's office to discuss me. Trisha was about 5-foot-8 and well over 300 pounds. She had one brown eye and one gray eye. The gray eye was legally blind because it turned gray from a faulty contact she once wore. I can't remember what she said, but I was extremely disturbed by her presence and her trying to paint a picture of me and prove how imperfect I was. At the end of the day, her efforts didn't work. Ms. King loved me and believed in me regardless of what people would say. That again turned into a lesson about love. Love is everlasting. Her love didn't change based on the ugly parts of me being exposed to her. However, it hurts my feelings to think about how someone would try to break one of the only genuine bonds that I had at the time in order to ensure I had nothing.

It wasn't long before other family members would come to stay with us either short- or long-term. One of those families would be my uncle's children and his baby's mom. The first day may have been pleasant. I was reminded that I met them all before when we were very young and though I didn't remember, I did believe the adults that said I had met the older ones when we were younger.

Sometime during my stay, my mother sent a watch to the house that my grandmother bought for me. It was a watch with the famous Precious Moments children in it. My cousin Anna was so fascinated with it that after having it briefly in my hand for 10 minutes, she asked to wear it for the day. Well, when I wasn't paying attention, Anna left the house. I would later find out that she'd given the watch to her boyfriend's sister and I never saw it again.

Anna and her boyfriend were over frequently. Yet when he came, so did at least two of his friends. So imagine the scene: Anna and her boyfriend were kissing and exchanging touches while the friends were looking around seeing who they could hook up with. I was not interested even a bit so though there were flirtatious gestures from there, I made it clear that I was not going to involve myself with any of them.

I was 16 at the time and Anna was at least a year younger than me, so I am still amazed to this day about what she'd get herself into. One day Anna decided she wanted to have sex. So she had my young cousins that I shared a room with to go sleep with their sister while her friends sat in the single bed (it was across from the bunk bed, on the side) and I slept (laid) in the bed below. There was no way I was going to sleep but I pretended to. No one would be able to sleep as the bed above was shaking, and all the noises that were associated with sex were happening. I was so fascinated with the whole situation! I knew I had to keep myself safe as there were two horny boys in the room with us watching the scene. I knew that sex with me was on their mind either consental or rape so I stayed very astute though to the naked eye I was sleeping. And to be completely transparent, I think this whole scene was a setup. Those boys could have waited in the living room or Anna could have chose to have sex somewhere where they could be alone. Yet I was stuck in this room on high guard with teenage boys that carried guns in their waistbands.

You might be wondering why I didn't simply go into the living room, I could have and initially I tried, yet I was pulled to the side by Anna and asked not to as Trisha would ask why I wasn't sleeping in the room and I would blow her cover. As wise as I was, I was still 16 and peer pressure got the best of me at that moment. Plus I figured that I could protect myself. I wasn't afraid. I was disgusted but I obliged.

As Anna slept with her boyfriend, his two friends sat in the single bed. When one of them thought I was asleep, he came in my bed and began to rub my leg. I was not about to see what would happen next so I hopped up and sat on the living room couch until the next morning. It is by the grace of God that nothing else happened to me as I was a fighter at this time and they had guns. I would not have allowed them to take my virginity without a fight, so I thank God that they didn't try to force me to sleep with them. I do believe that God has always covered me! Though there were some extremely trying times, I think I've always had a hedge of protection around me where God has allowed humans to do their human thing but only to a certain extent.

This incident, as odd as it was, wasn't really out of place for Trisha's house. I was introduced to porn in this house. I remember one day all of the older cousins and my little brother were all glued to the TV. I was shocked and dismayed to see that they were watching the most grotesque porn. It was in black and white and the women were drinking cum from a cup! I couldn't believe what I was seeing and even more that they were all enjoying it together. I quickly exited stage left and let them enjoy the rest of their evening.

It didn't take long before all the girls and my little brother decided that it was time to gang up on me and for my cousin (Anna's younger sister) Francesca to fight me. I ignored them until one day we all ended up in the basement. I can't remember why we ended up down there. I think I decided that it was time to finally face the bully. What I do know is that Francesca told my little brother that she couldn't fight me without being angry so he had to make her mad. So he started to blurt out things like, "Yo' mama a crackhead...you ain't got nowhere to live..." until she pushed me and after that it was on! I beat Francesca's butt! At some point during the fight I got some super-human strength and picked Francesa up and threw her to the floor (I think it was all of my pent-up hurt and anger). Once she was on the floor, I continued to kick and stomp her until she kicked me in my vagina. At that point I was done because that hurt too much to play off. I made it back upstairs and I thought I was done.

All the kids ran to Trisha's room to discuss what happened and I was shocked to learn that I would be punished for fighting. To make matters worse, I had to all of a sudden do a load of clothes as ordered by Trisha. So I went back down to the basement to find Francesca behind the door and before I knew it, she punched me dead in my eye. I immediately ran upstairs and noticed the skin around my eye was red and swollen. It would soon turn black. She had given me a black eye! I was so upset as I had school in the morning and tried to keep my school life separate from my home life. I raced to the freezer to try to bring the swelling down and hoped to God that he'd take away the darkness around my eye. At some point, Trisha called me into her room because she said she had questions but when I entered she pointed and laughed at my eye and that solidified that hate I had for her.

By this time I was so frustrated and sometimes I'd vent to Trisha's then 12-year-old child, her only daughter-Bria. At 12, she seemed to have an understanding of a lot of things. One day we were in her room crying over our lives. I told Bria that sometimes to assuage myself I'd cut myself. I told her that I did it because I was able to control my hurt. So we went into the bathroom and I got the razor blades but Bria chickened out. I told her that I was extremely suicidal and I should take the pills and end my life. At this point, Bria ran into her mother's room crying and telling her what I wanted to do to myself. Trisha came into the bathroom and said, "Just kill yourself then." And at that moment, all the desire to kill myself dissipated. I thought I wanted to die but when someone else doesn't care about you, it gives you a desire to live, or at least it did for me.

In addition to the roaches that ran rampant in Trisha's house, she also had mice that creeped me out! One day I had a Now and Later that got stuck in the carpet. I didn't think anything of it after I tried to get it out the carpet to no avail. Imagine my surprise to wake up in the middle of the night to see mice fighting over it! I was terrified but I had to use the restroom so badly so I hurried up and hit the light on and watched mice jump behind dressers. Before going back to sleep, I drowned the Now and Later with dishwashing liquid in order to make the mice not smell or want it. It worked to keep them off the candy, but they were still everywhere in that house.

Thanksgiving that year was a day where I felt more hateful than thankful. The day started off like any other but Trisha's two young sons had a fascination with hitting me. This day in particular I was tired of telling them to stop. I went to Trisha to ask her to tell them to stop and she told me that their baby hands weren't hurting me. As they continued, I began to tap their hands to tell them to stop. They'd then tell on me. Trisha told me not to touch her kids and I asked her to tell her kids to stop hitting me. She ignored me. When they hit me again and I tapped their hand back, Trisha came into the room and got in my face and told me not to touch her kids. I started to yell back and get in Trisha's face. Though Trisha was three times my size, I didn't care. When I got to my breaking point, I had no logic. This time her daughter came to back her up and I had both of them in my face threatening me to do something.

At this point I darted out of the house feeling so angry. I remember chanting as I trekked the 10 blocks to my Aunt Carolyn's house "I hate everybody except...". I did not pay attention to street lights and I had no fatigue. If I got hit by a car, it wouldn't have mattered. I made it to my aunt's house and broke down crying telling her what Trisha did to me. She wiped my eyes, went outside and called Trisha on the pay phone. The conversation went something like, "You AIDS-having bitch... put your hands on my niece and imma beat your ass."

My brother Garland had stopped by and they filled him in. After that I was so mentally exhausted I fell asleep. Hours later my aunt woke me up to tell me that Trisha said I must come home immediately or she'd file a missing person's report and report my aunt for kidnapping. My brother volunteered to take me home.

When we arrived, he confronted Trisha. He told her that if she put her hands on me, she'd have to deal with him. I watched Trisha stand there and say nothing. She knew he meant every word and for the first time in a long time, I felt protected.

After that exchange, Bria and my other cousins told me that they were sorry and left me some pie from the dinner I wasn't able to partake in. I thanked them and went into the room. Not too long later they brought the pie and told me to try it. I wanted to believe they had good intentions so I tried the pie and it wasn't bad. Immediately they all started laughing and let me know that the pie fell on the floor and they then placed it in the refrigerator for me to eat.

No one allowed me space in that house and I was constantly fighting. This time it involved my cousin's mother. I remember calling her a crackhead and her telling me my mother was one. That was the last day I had anything to do with her. I cussed her out with all my might and got in trouble for cussing. Everyone in that house cussed and I only did when I got mad. For everyone else, no one batted an eye but for me it always resulted in a punishment.

My younger brother wanted in on the action too. One day he decided he wanted to fight me. This is where I drew the line and I refused to fight my brother. I remember him trying to aggravate me and try to pull me off the couch to fight him. I realized at this point how anatomically boys were stronger than girls. My brother was born a year and month after me, but he was so much stronger. I resorted to cussing him out and Trisha resorted to punishing me. This time I didn't care and we cussed each other out all night. When Trisha had enough, she proudly called my father and told him to get his unruly daughter. Trisha was most excited to see me in trouble. My dad came and took me to his house. He asked what happened and left it at that. There, I'd stay on his couch.

He and his wife did their own thing and I did mine. I was only responsible for washing my clothes. I'd get myself up in the morning and go to school. I'd come home, do my homework and watch television until I fell asleep. His wife braided my hair a couple times during my stay and my dad watched a few shows with me. I was so numb at this point that I was merely living day to day. Yet I was very happy on my father's couch with no one to bother me. That was until Trisha got upset that I didn't want to come home and had my father take me back to her house for more torture.

For my birthday that year my father bought me a beanie baby Noah's Ark. It was a paper boat filled with 2 beanie babies of several animals. I cherished that gift as I thought it was so cute. One thing I also enjoyed doing was recording on blank tapes. I liked to tell myself how I was feeling and sing myself songs that I wrote. I mistakenly took one of Bria's tapes that was one of her favorite artists and recorded over it. I thought it was a regular blank tape. When she found out, I apologized and told her that as soon as I got money, I'd buy her a new one. I never got the chance.

The next day I came home to my beanie babies thrown around the room and out the window. My Noah's Ark boat was completely ripped and I had a trophy I earned from the Mary Ryan's Boys and Girls Club broken in half. I found out that Trisha told Bria to do these things because I recorded on her tape. The truth is that Trisha was jealous of my accomplishments and my gift and was looking for an opportunity to hurt my feelings. Well it worked because she and her daughter absolutely did as well as destroy irreplaceable things for an accident that I could very well fix for $5.00.

One thing is for sure, God was ever present even then. My bed was right by the window and one day I noticed that the window didn't lock. I looked out of it once and saw the largest rat I ever saw rummaging through garbage. I told God I hope he never made it in the house. One day as I was sleeping, I felt the window come open. As I opened my eyes, I saw the hands lifting it up. I ran to the living room and sat quietly just as I did the night of the attempted rape. This time my brother LJ (Lloyd) was sleeping on the couch and it wasn't long before he woke up and asked me why I wasn't in bed. When I explained to him why he told me to sleep on the couch and he'd sleep in the bed. My brother is now deceased but I have several precious memories of being protected by him and I thank God for his sweet, always protective soul.

That Christmas, my former foster mother Maria invited me over. Not too long later we agreed that I'd come back to live there. The day I left my things weren't packed so she told Trisha we'd come the next day. She set a time and we left. The next day we came at that time and Trisha refused to answer the door. There was a special metal box and it had all that was left of my prized possessions. Trisha knew that. I had all my writings and awards and written goals dating as far back as elementary school. I am certain she withheld it on purpose and destroyed it.

Ch.9

TRANSITION TO TRANSITIONAL HOUSING

The second time I stayed at Maria's house wasn't long. I began to have problems getting along with her soon after I got back.

It was the second and last time I was kicked out of Maria's house. This time, I headed to a group home. Maria told the social workers that I was not to return to the house and they were to pick me up from school. Unbeknownst to me at that time (Charisma would tell me years later), Ms. King had called my friends in the office and told my best friends at the time, Riley and Charisma, to go easy on me. She went on to tell them that I may be easily angered and may lash out on them unmerited but to be patient with me and understanding as my life was forever changing.

So I waited after school to be picked up and Ms. King waited with me. I didn't ask her to wait but through the years she has always had the intuition to know what to do when I needed it most. That day I experienced something that I hadn't experienced prior. She held me and allowed me to cry in her arms. We didn't exchange any words and though I was extremely sad and terrified, I knew I'd be OK. Her love renewed me. In my mind I wanted to feel like I didn't have love based on my circumstance but she totally diverted that thought. I will never forget how she made me feel that day. Ms. King would always give hugs to everybody and was always loving but this was different. I felt individual. I felt special. I finally felt like I mattered to someone. That day was the first day that I can remember what I felt like to feel deep, undeniable, maternal love. It was exactly what I needed before I went to my next destination.

I was 17 and terrified. I was being placed in a home for troubled girls and I felt very much like a prisoner. Furthermore I was informed that we could only take seven outfits to our room. There were no appliances upstairs (TV, radio, etc.) and when we were together (other than the bedrooms) we moved as a unit. Therefore, we all had to be in the same room at the same time. If one person had to use the restroom, we were to wait in the hallway so that we could all be supervised. In the kitchen there were no knives, only spoons and forks. They felt that we could be a danger to ourselves or others if we were allowed the opportunity to have them so they were not permitted.

I remember thinking about how I cared about school and being successful and that I would be with girls who lacked those same ambitions. Though I trusted God to protect me, I knew I'd face opposition and I'd be fresh meat to these girls.

The first days were interesting to say the least. I sat down with an intake counselor. I was supposed to inventory every item of clothing I had but she told me that it was unnecessary because only the adults would be allowed in the basement to retrieve clothes. That was mistake number one. We were allowed one special item to place in a glass china cabinet for quick access. Many opted to keep their toiletries but I placed my jewelry box in that cabinet. It was special to me. My foster mother Maria had bought it for me for Christmas when I was in third grade. It came with a gold bracelet that had my name engraved in it. The jewelry box had a windup ballerina that played the most calming classical tune. Many days I enjoyed spinning her up and using the box less so for jewelry but more so for notes and special items I saved.

Many days roll into one in my memories. I spent about 3 months there. However, when drama unfolded, they were anything but ordinary. Other than meeting with my intake counselor to not label my clothes and to sign a contract that stated that I would be in at a certain time each day, go to school and follow their rules with a promise of a small allowance weekly, that's all I remember about the first day. Yet I began to encounter many young ladies who have had a lasting impact on my life.

Connie was the manifestation of what I felt on the inside. She was quiet and not the most attractive, and because of those qualities, she became a target. There was this time we were all in the living room (as we were required to always be together). One young lady decided to discuss how something didn't smell good. "Somebody stank," she began to taunt. Then she began to ask us all if we smelled it. I told her I did not but some agreed it did and that it was Connie. I have a very sensitive nose and I didn't smell her.

This conversation went on the entire time in the living room. Then as we were going to bed it continued. This particular night (prior to the smell allegations), Connie and I made a connection. She told me how she ended up in the foster system. She detailed how her mother suffered with mental health issues. She said she was able to see spiritually. She explained that that day she saw a demon jump out of her mom and enter some of the bodies that were in the house.

That was also the day her mother lost it. She said her mother threw one of her siblings down a flight of stairs and violently physically abused the rest of them. I was so captivated by her story that we continued to talk upstairs.

Prior to that connection, I had also connected with another young lady. I was beginning to see that this experience was bigger than me. The girls were not intimidated by me but sought me out as someone to vent to and get spiritually affirmed. I would share my sorrows but always point to Christ. He was the one whom I told them I relied on, and who gave me the strength to endure.

Upstairs was dedicated to bedtime solely. That is why there were no electronics allowed there. There were four rooms with two beds in each room. There was also a sitting area. The sitting area was reserved for the lady who supervised us at night but the workers who were supposed to supervise us never came up. They'd stay downstairs and watch television and we rarely went to sleep right away.

After the majority of the girls declared that Connie smelled, she wanted to debrief with me. She told me that she used to be extremely angry ...so angry they put her in anger management. She said she learned to count down and ignore negativity. That was how she was able to ignore the allegations of not smelling fresh. She said she would count down in her head and by the time she got to one, she didn't feel intensely angry and it distracted her from what was said.

As I was taking in what Connie was saying, another young lady, Tisha, decided to come into the room and taunt Connie. She told her she smelled and she was too old to smell, etc. Connie turned to me and ignored Tisha. Tisha didn't like that and tried to coerce me into bullying Connie with her, but I decided to engage with Tisha. As the taunting intensified Connie began to count out loud. Her classes were working perfectly until while Connie was counting down, Tisha decided to punch Connie in the mouth. Blood immediately began to drip from Connie's mouth. That is when positive Connie abandoned all she had learned.

I sat on the bed in shock. Connie was silent. She got up and went straight to the kitchen. Tisha stayed in my room with a smile. As Connie came back upstairs she presented a fork (we had no knives specifically for this reason). They began to fight outside my door and I closed my door. I remember picking up the phone and calling Mrs. Evans and telling her I was so scared because it was a knock-down, drag-out fight happening in the hallway. She asked why I was telling her and not getting the adult in charge. On the other side of the door I heard banging and knocking but seeing the fight didn't interest me.

Once all the noise ended I opened the door to a horrific scene. There were knocked over lamps and two bloodied teenagers. That fork was on the floor bent in half! On both of their bodies was evidence that they used the fork to harm each other as they both had fork lines on some part of their body.

By this time the supervising adult came up and the fight was over. The police were on their way. Tisha had a big smile on her face while Connie was very angry. Tisha came in the room and tried to hug me before she left in handcuffs but I told her no because she was bleeding (and I did not know if she had AIDS). I did tell Connie goodbye as she was leaving in handcuffs however. They had to arrest both girls until they found out who started what. We would have to stay up to give our account and there were many nights like this!

Anytime there was any extraordinary activity, we were up until 2 or 3 in the morning and I still faithfully got up and went to school as if I did not live the life that I did. I had a very small circle of friends and even fewer knew what I went home to in my junior year of high school. It was a surreal experience and I lived in two worlds. I was an honor roll student at a private Catholic school by day and a child thrown away at night.

They would later release Connie to a foster home that was waiting for her. Tisha was not as lucky. Tisha and I had just had a conversation about the new prospective foster home she'd be going to before she decided to bully Connie. Once her potential foster parents heard she was a bully, they decided they didn't want her and she'd have to stay in the juvenile detention center and possibly a more restrictive girl's home until they could find a placement. I knew how much that meant to Tisha as she was very excited to be a part of a family, but I felt what she did was out of order so I did not have that much sympathy for her at that time.

I penned this poem for Connie after the event before knowing what her outcome would be:

Dear Connie (written March 12, 2003)

If I could tell you that I understood
Would it do any good?
Would it have stopped you from jeopardizing you?
Would it have helped what you were going through?
Well the truth is - I feel for you
I know
There is nothing like being lonely
Coming home to a house not a home
Being fearful but afraid to express it
Having pain but continually repressing it
I saw from the beginning
When I looked into your eyes
All the nights you secretly cried
I heard in your voice when you (were) defending yourself
How much you hid on the shelf
I felt the names from the pain you were called
I saw myself feeling so small
You tell me what I could've been
When I wanted to be negative
And if (they) only listened
Oh the things you could give
The life you could lead
The dreams you hold
You just have to believe

I will never forget the youngest child I saw enter Positive Pathways (the group home/girl's shelter). Her name was Rose. Aretha Franklin had a song that said, "A rose is still a rose...baby girl you're still a flower...he can leave you and break you...darling you hold the power"... and Rose embodied every bit of that song.

Rose came into the facility looking for love. She was small in frame and stature, light skinned with her hair shaved really low on her head(it was obvious her haircut was from her hair not being taken care of). She was only 12 years old. She would lay on any of the other girls' laps or chests at any time during the day. She wanted to be held and loved on. Each day I'd leave for school, and the other girls would leave for merriment. I was the only child who actually went to school but the facility didn't care. They wanted us out each day so they gave us two bus tickets each morning and made sure they reminded us that they better not see us during school hours. They knew these young ladies were not attending school, but we were kids where doing the minimum was acceptable. As long as we had transportation, food and a place to sleep, social services was OK.

Rose decided to hang with the truants. These girls enjoyed being entertained by men. They would sleep with these men and make money to get their hair and nails done and that is who Rose attached herself to. Rose was not there very long before she told the girls she was going with them one school morning. However, when they came home that night, Rose was not with them. They were very nonchalant about it. They said that she decided to entertain men alone and they left her at the library. So here we were again, up late on a school night once Rose did not make it in before curfew.

They started a police search. Days went by and there were no signs of Rose. The winter time complicated their search as people were not really outdoors so spotting her outside was nearly impossible. About a week went by and finally we received notice that they had found Rose! Yet Rose was not OK! They found her with no coat or shoes on and she did not know her name! She couldn't tell where she had been and what was done to her. Whatever happened to her was so traumatic that she did not remember the encounter. I was so shaken by this experience that I wrote this short reflective poem/song in her honor:

Rose
*Would a Rose by Any Other Name Smell as Sweet?
All she wanted was love
And found pain at her feet
Now I don't know Rose too well
But as far as I could Tell
All She Ever Wanted Was Love

*(first line adapted from Romeo and Juliet by William Shakespeare)

Not too long after that incident I had a roommate and this girl smelled for real...well, her shoes did. She was a white girl named Kami who stayed to herself. But that first night together, we bonded. She told me her story. She described that she grew up pretty normally until her mother's sudden and tragic suicide. That is when she went to live with her sister who was in her early 20s. She described how even that environment was OK until one day her sister woke up and said, "I can't do this," and drove her sister to the social services building. Which was how she ended up in the facility.

This facility we lived in was a house that they turned into a group home/shelter for foster girls in transition.

From the outside it looked like any other house but the neighborhood knew exactly what the facility was and that was embarrassing to me as I trekked to the bus stop each day. I imagined that the onlookers were judging and looking down on me and while some of them maybe were, most were in their own state of poverty that comes with its own issues and probably cared less about what I was doing there. That facility was like a scarlet letter. That facility was for girls no one wanted at the time. It was a holding cell until they could beg a foster family to take you in lieu of your issues.

As Kami began to tell her story, she expressed to me that she was atheist. I explained to her that while I could not totally relate to her experience with her mother, my mother and I were estranged and I suffered every type of abuse in the hands of the foster system but one thing I knew was that God was real! I told her that I had this CD by India Arie with this song I wanted her to hear. So she snuck up a CD player and I snuck up my CD to play the track, "God is Real" for her. India had this line that repeated that expressed, "That's how I know that God is real... all of this is not by chance." I explained to her that despite all that I had been through and the state of depression I was in, I knew God was real and working on my behalf. I had witnessed too many of his miracles in spite of all the pain I had endured.

We talked for hours that night and that is when Kami revealed that she was "going AWOL in the morning," but she thought she now believed in God! I tried to convince her not to run away but I was so grateful that my testimony inspired her in that way. I still get emotional over that! This experience was God using me. Each girl came to me with a story randomly and while I witnessed them abuse each other, they never tried to fight or even argue with me. God gave me an aura of sorts and so each girl only wanted to talk and receive counsel from me. At the time I didn't see it like that. I chalked these things up to random occurrences but I now know that God had allowed this experience to increase my faith as I was increasing the faith of those around me.

The next day, Kami did exactly what she said she would do. I tried to stop it. I went to the staff to let them know. They told me that they could not prevent her from leaving. Kami had somehow got her bag of clothes and she was out the door. I never saw her again, but I will never forget that short but powerful experience we shared.

Then there was Savayla. I thought she was breathtakingly beautiful. She was 16, thin, with caramel skin and medium-length relaxed hair. Yet her past was anything but beautiful. She described how her mother passed away while she was very young and therefore they gave custody to her father. She later learned that he was her younger brother's biological father, not hers. He had been molesting her since she was a small child.

The way that Savayla discovered that she was being molested was shocking. She had started to attend school and through a casual conversation with her teacher, she revealed the details of how her father would molest her. She was too young to know about sex and molestation and learned that what her father was doing was wrong through that encounter.

By the time I met Savayla she was 16 and had been in many foster homes. She told me about the hopes of finding a forever family. She discussed how if she was given another opportunity that she would "be good" and "follow the rules." She was so hopeful and optimistic that she would find a forever home because she would do everything she could to maintain her placement.

Savayla did not stay at the group home long and I was happy to see her go and get the life she desperately needed and wanted. I remember having a conversation with her before she left where she told me about her new family. She exclaimed, "I have a mom **and** a dad! I am so excited and I am going to be good!" I ended up seeing Savayla a couple years post group home and after exchanging hugs I had to get an update on her experience with her family.

To my disappointment and hers, she detailed how the mom-and-dad dynamic was just a facade. She went on to say that the father created a military style living environment. Everyone was responsible for getting up early and cleaning up. After that, they were to exit the house and not return until a certain time later that evening. She said despite that she was still trying to make the placement work. Yet she began to see stark differences in how she was treated as opposed to their biological adult children. She told me how she watched them celebrate their adult children's birthdays with so much pomp and circumstance that she waited to see what festivities would await her. However she expressed that all she got was a new pajama set and there were no celebrations for her.

That broke my heart. I knew how desperately she wanted to be loved. By the time I was 16, I was no longer seeking love from my foster parents but respect and acceptance. I didn't want hugs or family time but I also didn't want to be treated as I didn't exist. So when I saw how innocent

Savayla still was and she still had a heart that was waiting for a family to love, cherish and accept her, I was confronted with the reality of the system that I knew too well. I still did not understand how adults could hurt a child intentionally by deliberately treating them poorly while collecting money on their behalf.

I haven't seen Savayla since then but I sincerely hope she found her forever family or that she's created a healthy, unified one of her own.

Just as stunningly beautiful as Savayla was, so was a hispanic girl named Reina. She was so spunky from the time she arrived. You could tell that she wanted to be accepted and to fit in badly and unfortunately that was to her detriment.

Reina spent her days running around the neighborhood doing God knows what and chasing stray cats. One night during Reina's stay, the girls invited me to the room to have a pow wow. It was there where Reina sought to dominate the conversation. She told us how she tried to take ownership of this stray cat to give it a home. Being kids we thought that was so hilarious and silly but now I can see that that stray cat may have seen herself in that cat. She was such a "soft" girl who wanted someone to give her security and love. We really were all strays.

That night, they decided to play a game with Reina. They told her to sit on the bed and once she sat down, they pulled both her and the cover off the bed. Each time she hit the floor with a thud and she laughed loudly and proudly when underneath I knew she was hurt. I walked out after about the fifth pull. I couldn't stand to see someone being hurt even if they pretended to like it.

The craziest fight I have ever seen in my life would have to be the battle of the pay phone. In the facility we had one house phone that we were granted access and it was a pay phone. Most of us did not have cell phones so this was our only communication with the outside world. One day one of the young ladies was not being respectful with time. A supervising adult was supposed to monitor our phone time but she found it much easier to let us fight over it, and fight over it they did! One moment they were yelling about whose turn it was and the next minute I saw the other girl being beaten with the pay phone. The police were called and this was another day I had to stay up late as they took statements from each of us. Looking back, I am amazed at how well I was able to go to school as if I hadn't experienced hell the night before. This would come in handy as I ventured through life.

The group home/shelter worked on a points system. You needed a certain amount of points to be able to go out on the weekends, and even more points to have overnights. I always had enough points but I rarely had anywhere to go and never had any house to sleep at overnight. One weekend I thought I was "living the good life". There was only one other girl there so the facility was so quiet and chill. Someone had given me some money and I went to the corner store to get some snacks. Everything was great until out of nowhere I started to regurgitate a huge pile of snacks. The ordeal weakened me and I remember the one other girl who was there that weekend was disgusted. So the supervising adult came in and told me I had to clean it up. I ventured to do so and threw up again and at that point she knew that the only way that vomit was coming out the carpet was if she cleaned it up. Imagine how upset she was and how I had to hear about how cleaning up my puke was not in her job description.

Everything wasn't late-night conversations and drama. We were not given any money therefore our hair looked like how experienced and creative we could be. I was good at this as I had to figure out how to deal with my hair since the age of 11. So one thing I did was braid some of their hair. All they had to do was buy the hair and I would do it. This was one way that I got to know the girls and pass the time.

I not only obtained favor among the girls but also obtained favor from many of the supervising staff. There are few incidents that stand out to me. There was this one girl who only stayed with us a really short time. On one of her first nights she observed how the staff allowed me in the kitchen alone or to even do small things like get them ice. So she asked me to sneak her cell phone upstairs since I was not checked and patted down like the other girls as "they knew I wouldn't sneak things upstairs." I agreed to but unbeknownst to us the staff saw the exchange. The supervising adult in charge played it so smoothly! She didn't say anything when it first happened, she did the normal pat-down routine to everybody and when it came to me she told everyone to go upstairs and for me to stay back. She told me that she saw me take her possessions upstairs and told me that I am a good girl and I ought not take the fall for someone else. She went on to say that she wouldn't take all my points which would limit my weekend privileges but if I was to do it again, she would. I was very grateful for that experience and the young lady whose phone was confiscated didn't even care that her phone was taken as much as she was relieved she didn't get caught with it. I think she assumed that I lost points that day and didn't even apologize. I always wanted to please people and I hope I learned to not take the fall for people because if they are asking you to, they are basically telling you that they would prefer you to suffer while they reap the benefits and you are verbally agreeing to be misused in that way and that is NOT OK.

One night while we were all supposed to be sleeping we heard so much commotion at the door. We heard the supervising adult screaming at someone at the door to leave. The kids told me that she owed her drug dealer money and he was trying to get through to get to her. This exchange went on for quite some time and whoever was at the door eventually left. I'm not sure if any of that was true but what I do know is she obviously was on something based on what she was about to do next.

The morning started off like every other morning. I got ready and was ready to head out the door. The rest of the girls were doing chores. We had this unwritten understanding that I wouldn't do chores because I needed to catch the bus in order to get to school on time. Well this day, the lady that had the battle with the guy at the door decided to bother me. She stopped me dead in my tracks as I was getting ready to head out the door and confronted me about not doing the chores. The girls intercepted the conversation and said things like, "Let her go. We do them because she actually goes to school." But she was not having it, and she said I could do a quick chore like take out the garbage.

I was so annoyed because up until this point I had only done chores at night. But I quickly grabbed the garbage and headed out the door. When I got to the garbage can, I was greeted by the shock of my life. My precious jewelry box, the one item I had left out for easy access, was sitting on top of the garbage. So I tried to retrieve it but I found that it was intentionally smothered in used cooking oil and other garbage. At this point I realized what was happening. This bitch had intentionally told me to take the garbage out so that she could get the satisfaction of hurting my feelings.

I would experience this several times on my journey! There were several adults who did not like my drive and my will to succeed so they would intentionally try to dampen my spirit as if it wasn't already hard to find hope. I completely believe this was spiritual.

After I saw that, I dropped the garbage and went into the house on fire! I was ready to go to jail after getting my hands on that woman! I went into the house to her snarl and immediately tried to lunge at her. I began to chase her around the table. The girls started to confront me asking, "What are you doing...what is going on?" I blurted out, "That bitch told me to take out the garbage because she threw my jewelry box away? She has to die."

Immediately they turned to her asking her, "Why did you do that?... She don't bother nobody!" She didn't respond to them, she simply picked up the work phone to call the police. I pulled the cord out from the wall so she got on her cell phone and called them. Eventually the girls stopped me and told me to go to school and they would handle her and I left because I realized that they had my back and school was everything to me. It was not only the place that would get me to access my dreams, but it was my peace. Ms. King and other supportive staff were there. I just needed to get to school.

While that was the worst of what I dealt with in terms of staff, I did have a small tiff with the owner of the home. I had been thinking about the contract I signed and I realized that we were supposed to receive an allowance weekly. I met with the other girls and realized that they hadn't really read the contract to know we had an allowance. I arranged a meeting with the director. She stayed in her office for hours that day. When she emerged she handed me my "original" contract. The only thing was the allowance clause was taken out. I was floored because I know what I read. I told her that she had Bibles in every room but clearly didn't follow or believe in the context. I told her that I knew she got thousands for each of us per month and for her not to give us the little bit of money owed was ungodly. She responded that she never said she was a Christian, that I had made an assumption and allowance was earned and given out once it was earned.

When I reached the age of 17.5 I was given the opportunity to leave Positive Pathways and to partake in what was known as independent living.

But before I left I had to go to the basement to get out all of my items. What I would find would shock me. My property was stolen! I had an Adidas dance outfit that was jogging pants, Adidas tennis shoes and the matching jacket (because I was on the dance team) that was gone. My former foster sister gave me a dress I was going to wear to prom (brand new) - gone! Basically all my nice clothes were gone. I realized that when the staff member that was responsible for intake told me not to inventory my stuff, it was because she had an eye on it. Since I didn't do inventory I had to suck it up. It was bittersweet. I was so happy to leave that it didn't really sink in that most of my stuff was gone but it would hit me and make me sad for years to come. It was less about the clothes but the sentimental value attached and the reality that someone would take my property when I trusted them to protect it.

The apartment I moved into was in downtown Milwaukee in a quiet neighborhood. Mrs. Evans would take me there. She was always transporting me somewhere at this stage in my life. She was the one making sure I had groceries, if I had no money, she gave me some. She made sure I always had the necessities I needed, always. Her family also wrapped around me and supported me. Her mom, Mrs. Wells, in particular, would randomly give me money and always made sure I ate after church on Sundays.

Ch.10

STEPPING INTO ADULTHOOD

Once I was all stocked and settled in Mrs.Evans hugged me, probably gave me some advice and she was off.

This was a suite apartment. That meant that there was an outside door that two people who shared a suite would share. They would also share a bathroom. My apartment did not have a full-size refrigerator as it literally was just a room. We had a mini-fridge in each room and at the end of the hall was a full kitchen, with a full refrigerator that everyone shared. This apartment complex had many different functions. My floor was dedicated to 17-year-old foster youth and women (usually younger women) who had a baby under 1 year old. I came to discover that the baby sides of the floors were much larger and they did not have suitemates.

Independent living felt glamorous to me...even in my small suite! On top of that, every week I received $300 to purchase my necessities. I didn't have any bills and I still worked a part-time job (Jewel-Osco) so in my teenage brain, I was basically rich. I wish someone would have advised me about credit and savings at that time but no one did. Now when I went to school, I felt so fly! People could not understand how I now had new tennis shoes every month but they did not ask, either.

My grades were straight A's that year. I had been an honor roll student my entire life but now I had an opportunity to focus on me! I didn't have to watch anyone else's kids, I didn't have to be privy to anyone's drama... All I had to do was focus on me and that gave me energy to pour into my schoolwork. Part of independent living was a program for the girls to meet with a counselor weekly to discuss a plan. No one took these meetings seriously, including me. The girls mostly weren't interested in their services and I was preparing for college. That did not matter to the women when I came to them one day and let them know that the meetings were hindering my chances to participate in cheerleading practice. I was frustrated and tried to honor the program then eventually said screw it and continued with my extra curriculars. When my first report card came, I had to let them know that they weren't dealing with the regular girls they were used to dealing with. I was a straight-A student so when I said I had duties after school that is what I meant! After that, their whole approach changed toward me and they laid off the extra responsibilities they were requiring.

Not too long after that, they told me that they wanted to feature me in the Journal Sentinel (the city's newspaper). I talked to Mrs. Evans about it as I felt that my story would embarrass me once my classmates found out that I grew up in the system and was currently living in independent living. However she reminded me that my story could heal or inspire someone in my situation, so I did it.

I was very excited about the interview until I realized that yellow journalism was a real thing. I thought the story was about me but the story was really highlighting the success story of independent living! That left me slightly offended because independent living only provided me shelter and as we know shelter was beneficial as it gave me the ability to focus on the things that were more important like my schooling. Yet in terms of my schooling, they could get no credit for that! That was my drive! I woke up every morning to ensure that I was on time. I made sure I got my homework done, no one else! Yet I took that one for the sake of inspiration and let it be!

The independent living program was my first step into adulthood and my first opportunity to make my own decisions. It also was a time in my life where I decided that I wanted to date or at least see if it interested me at that point.

One of the other perks of independent living was the independence! It didn't take me long to realize that if I made a mistake there was no parent to discipline me! I didn't seek to get in trouble, but that felt great. That same year (junior year) I tested my luck and that could've ended it all for me. We had a policy at Messmer where only one student could go to the restroom at a time during lunch and you'd have to surrender your ID so that the teachers could keep track of who was gone. My friends wanted us to go together so we decided to sneak there. Catholic schools are good at maintaining order and we did not make it very far without being caught. Once we got caught, we were ordered to report to the principal's office.

I was annoyed because they were so harsh and one teacher in particular told another teacher, "Escort them to the office!" Of course I felt really grown so I told him, " Dang I know where the office is... I don't need an escort."

That was all the ammunition they needed and the next thing I knew, I was suspended. In the report it detailed that I was belligerent to the point of using profanity at several teachers which did not happen.

When I was called back days later I had a meeting with the assistant principal Donna Childs. While Ms. Child's role in my life was small... It was extremely significant. Anytime you visited Ms. Childs, she had a smirk/smile on her face no matter what you had done. I often asked her about that and I can't remember exactly what she said but it was something along the lines of her being a happy person naturally and our consequences may dissatisfy her but didn't necessarily anger her. I enjoyed her so much because she was firm but fair. The way she loved was different but necessary. It was calming but very real.

Sitting on that hard bench outside her office let me know that I was in trouble in some form or fashion and I remember the few times I had to sit on that bench watching the others before me and being terrified of what was to come.

This conversation was my re-entry conversation. I would have to present myself before a few teachers, the principals and president of the school and detail why I was an asset to the school. She let me know that all of the administration and several of the teachers had met about my next steps. She told me there were a few who were upset and I was not to speak about what happened and how the allegations were untrue but how I was an asset to the school. She also let me know that while I was on academic probation for the next year, it was more a scare tactic to keep me in line as they knew I had no guardian. I was never a problem before and I didn't plan to be one after so I was disturbed but not perturbed about the "threat".

With me "feeling myself" and stepping into what it meant to be a woman, there was a young man who had been pursuing me. I think I met him outside my school at the bus stop. He was fairly attractive and respectable enough that I thought I'd give him a chance. I always had some barriers to entertaining boys. One barrier was I'd ask them, "What did you see in me that made you interested?" This typically was followed by giggles and a, "You different." That usually made me roll my eyes but I'd still entertain the conversation until the "You a freak?" question would come up. That would be my last time I talked to them. Sometimes I'd start the conversation off with , Just so you know, I'm not having sex with you." They'd all agree that that wasn't their objective but many would soon find a way to leave the conversation or they'd entertain that conversation for that day but never call me back. I was 100% OK with that because I really did not want someone whose main objective was to have sex with me, especially because it wasn't going to happen.

All the other guys had failed the test but this guy, Shalamar, passed the first round. We talked on and off and each time I'd get off the phone and try to examine my heart. Do I like him? I did not know at that point and I was definitely guarding my heart. One day he brought up the idea of a date. Though nervous, I was excited to see what dating was all about. I let him know that I was fine with dating but I was a "queen" and I wasn't meeting him anywhere...he'd have to come to me or we'd meet in a mutual location. He said that was fine. I explained that I had my own place but we'd have to "date" in the lobby. I do not remember if I told him that I couldn't bring him back if I wanted to, but it didn't matter because he wasn't going up there even if I could. In the lobby was a TV and we watched a program. Shortly into the program, he tried to come in close and rub my hand, and I let him know that no touching whatsoever was allowed and he respected that. It was my senior year and he had asked me for a senior pic. I told him he could have one but he specifically wanted a "full-body pic." This was when I had a very slim waist, flat stomach and big hips so after the date I walked him to the bus stop and waited until it arrived. It was winter and we had on big puffy coats. He asked if we could have a side hug and I allowed him that and he seemed satisfied. Subsequently, he called me and planned a couple of dates. Each time he'd say he was coming and didn't. There weren't many of those before I completely disregarded him...at least for the time being.

Aside from his pursuit, I had my first experience with a lesbian trying to coax me. Because I was molested by a woman, masculine lesbian women always make me a bit nervous anyhow. In the presence of masculine lesbians, I feel like a little girl on the inside. It is truly a strange thing how our body processes trauma. Anyhow, I had ordered pizza one night and a lady who identified as lesbian was the pizza gal. After giving me my pizza and paying her, she said something really quickly at an extremely low tone. She was exactly the type of lesbian who intimidated me. She had slicked-back braids, and she was heavier-set but short. I asked her once to repeat herself and to not appear rude after the second time I said, "OK." What I didn't know was that I had agreed that she could call me! We hadn't exchanged numbers, she had taken my number from the delivery order. That night she called me and in a panic I hung up. She called me and called me (there was no caller-id attached to the phone) and I finally answered without hanging up. In that call she cussed me out and told me I shouldn't have said she should call if I didn't want to talk to her. I do not think I explained myself as I probably was too afraid to rebut but I learned to never agree or just simply reply "OK" if I did not hear what was said.

In terms of phones, I liked practical jokes and playing on the phones was something that I sometimes did with my friends. This particular day, my friend Melanie was over and we decided to call the dating line that always appeared on TV at night. We gave each other fake names and pretended to be in a love affair with the men on the other line. We found this to be hilarious as we could hear the excitement in their voices! This was big to me as this was my first time exploring sexually explicit content. What I did not know is that my suitemate had company over and she and her friend were listening at the door. She didn't know it was a joke so a few days later her friend (both of whom I had never said anything to besides "hi" to) asked me if I was gay. While I was struck by this question, it didn't take me long to see the correlation to why she was asking me this question and I flat out said , "No!" which was followed by roars of laughter. Part of me felt compelled to explain what we had done but I realized that I did not know her and did not care to explain. Once I told my friend, she decided that I needed to say something back and I agreed and she'd be the spokesperson. She called my suitemates house phone and went off on them saying things like "Ain't nobody gay over here... so y'all can stop with that witcho baldheaded ass." Looking back it was so unnecessary but hey, we were 17.

My friend and my suitemate went at it for a while until I snatched the phone and hung it up. They tried to call back to no avail. Then they came over and began banging on the door but we refused to open it up (I was not a fighter unless provoked and since I wasn't pushed, I wasn't going to open my door to trouble). I called the front desk on my suitemate and they advised her and her friend to leave us alone and end the madness. I was so nervous to open my door the next day for school but all was quiet.

However, upon arriving home, I was met by the door to my room being egged. At this point I went off and for the first time we had an exchange of words with each other. Of course I was gay and she was a broke baby mama(insert rolled eyes)! I eventually called the police on her. Once they arrived and heard us both out, they asked the facility to separate us and because she had a baby, they thought it was easier to move me so down I went to the other end of the hall and that was our last interaction with each other because we were in jeopardy of getting kicked out pending another major upheaval.

On a lighter note, prom season came and though it was my junior year, I decided to go. I had no clue how to figure everything out but I was determined to make it work for myself. I told Ms. King about my plans and she said, "Go to Mayfair Mall, find a dress and put it in my name...make sure it's not too expensive." That was that. I wasn't given a particular limit but I was certainly not about to get an expensive dress and disrespect the opportunity she gave me. So my friend and I went to Mayfair, slightly nervous about finding an inexpensive dress I actually liked but just like God always does, He showed up! I ended up finding a magenta form-fitting dress filled with sparkles for only $30 on clearance. I couldn't believe the price! I left it under Ms. King's name and went to find some shoes. I ended up purchasing some silver sandals and a silver purse from Payless that I was content with.

Everything came together. My friend's sister did my hair for free and some of my friends decided to rent a limo. The day of prom I went to Mrs. Evans' house and she did my makeup. It was a team effort but we all pulled it off.

On the way to prom, I felt on top of the world! We rode in a Suburban stretch limo and we got to drink soda out of wine glasses. We swore we were living! When I stepped into the Milwaukee Public Museum, I was met with gasps from everyone! They ran up to me, requested pictures and ogled at my presence. I was popular for a day and I loved it. It was one of the first times I felt exceptionally pretty and I had a great night. I didn't care that I didn't have a date because the friends I went with also didn't have one.

After prom was interesting. Several of us partygoers decided to go out to eat. The food was fine. I believe we went to Denny's or IHOP that evening. When we got the bill we were able to diplomatically assign the charges and everyone put it in the center of the table. There was one girl who decided to take the money and count it. What we didn't know was that she intended to steal the money so her and her boyfriend could get a hotel and that is what she did. She literally counted it, looked at us and said, "I'll pay y'all back" and ran! So to not be arrested, we also ran! I think most of my classmates didn't care because they enjoyed the thrill of the evening but I was pissed! She took my money and now this establishment and waitress would get nothing! Not to mention there are already stigmas around black teens frequenting establishments and doing things of this sort and here we were!

Following that night, we were all back in school and I wanted so desperately to tell our assistant principal. We attended a Catholic school and that was definitely grounds for expulsion. But I was asked not to. She never paid us back and I held resentment in my heart for a long time toward her. I still can't laugh about it. It was wrong in so many ways.

Along the same lines of getting dolled up and adored was an opportunity to be a part of a cotillion. I applied and was accepted but I had no way to know what I was getting myself into. A cotillion consisted of mandatory community service hours, weekly ballroom dance practices (with both a beau and father/father figure), purchasing a wedding dress and accessories, etiquette classes, etc. The cotillion acts as a symbol of a young woman's "coming out" or an intro to adulthood, and boy did I transform in ways that I could not have imagined. This cotillion also involved a pageant and opportunities for scholarship awards.

If I had known everything that it entailed, I am not sure I would have done it. The blessing was that I went in blindly so once I was involved, I was determined to make it to the finish line. It did not take long for the girls to see that I was very different from them. Most of them were middle class and all of them had a full team behind the scenes ensuring that they had everything they needed. Yet just like God, he had a "ram in the bush" ...several of them, actually.

The cotillion experience spans several months. It started in the spring and we had our formal coming out that November.

It started out simple enough. In the beginning ...for the first couple of months, it was just weekly practices with us girls. That was my first hurdle but a minor one. I had to catch the bus and the bus wasn't always on time and I had to take multiple buses. I couldn't simply take an earlier bus because we were using a school building and the dance coach had the key. Therefore no one was there early and she arrived on time. Everyone else arrived in their parents' warm cars and I was so embarrassed. I tried to avoid looking at the other girls as often I stood outside or walked to and from the bus but I was definitely in my head. I thought about how they must've felt like I was a poor unloved girl. That is how I felt about myself so I assumed that that is how everyone else felt as well. Eventually when the practices started to take place at night, one of the cotillion coordinators would take me home or send me in a cab.

The next hurdle was the dance with the beaus. We were to choose one either it being a boyfriend or a friend that was a boy. I had neither so they provided one for me. We had no chemistry or connection so it was simply a dance partner. I can imagine as I reflect that I was standoffish. He definitely didn't talk to me either so it was an awkward practice each time. As fate would have it, I overheard him say something disparaging about me as I walked up and so I immediately ran down the stairs to cry. I again was so embarrassed but it was as if my hurt was leading me. I couldn't believe I was running but I did. Several girls trailed behind me to see what was the matter and when I told them they swore that it was a misunderstanding. I am not sure if it was or not, but imagine dancing with my beau after that! Awkward! But we made it work.

The next challenge showed up in the form of a wedding dress. I knew it was something I could not afford and it wasn't something I was willing to ask for. By this time, the coordinators knew what was up, they picked me and another girl from the court up and had a dress fitting with several dress options at their house. We were able to pick a dress to borrow and we even were awarded pearls (as this was an AKA cotillion- the first african american greek sorority- Alpha Kappa Alpha). I felt beautiful in my dress and that crisis was averted quickly.

Up next was the dance with my father. Well, I was not going to ask my father so the closest man to me was Mrs. Evans' husband. He was always kind to me and played a large role at the church we attended. We had many conversations in passing or during church events but we did not have a deep personal relationship ourselves. Being the kind man that he was when I asked Mrs. Evans to ask him... he said yes. I do not know if he knew he'd have to attend so many practices and what his role entailed fully but we made it work and it was a unique experience for me but it wasn't awkward.

Part of our debutante experience was to be social and to have fun. I will never forget when we had a talent show! One of the young ladies decided to sing a song and dedicated it to me. It was "God Bless The Child" by Billie Holiday. I don't know how much I showed it on my face but that song really touched me. I was on my own in many ways and they could see it. I didn't thank her then but very recently I hit her up and let her know that I was so grateful for that dedication. I sincerely thank God for blessing me!

I didn't win any awards or even get a shout out in the advertisement portion of our bulletin, but I felt and was beautiful that night. I strolled that runway with everything that was in me and I participated in a life-altering experience that made me more of a woman, stronger and more ambitious to take this life by storm even if the opportunities and tools don't appear to be there! God uses all of our experiences, and I needed that cotillion.

Not only did I have support from amazing teachers and administrators at school, I also had people in my church community support me. There was this one couple in particular, the Macons, who would pick me up and drop me off from church. The husband in particular was extremely nice. He kept volunteering to teach me how to drive at no expense. On one hand, I was excited for the opportunity as my foster mother forbade us from learning to drive and getting a license at 16 as she didn't want any liabilities or responsibilities as it related to that matter. Yet I would learn that his motives weren't the purest which would show up about a year later.

While my junior and senior year were filled with me walking into adulthood. It did not come without its tears. Graduation was a major accomplishment as I was the first to graduate high school in my family! My parents hadn't done it and I do not believe their parents had either, so I may have been the very first to ever have from my bloodlines! While Mrs. Evans, my foster mom Maria, some of my siblings, cousins and even nephews and nieces came to my graduation, I had no party. That hurt my feelings severely that I fought to succeed, that I got into every college I had applied to with scholarships attached and yet no one threw me a celebration. I would find myself with mixed emotions several times when the events should've been happy. Those were the times when I knew my place. Those were the times when it was apparent there was no parental involvement. It was in no one's mind to celebrate me in that way because I wasn't theirs and therefore that hurt profusely.

I was asked to give the prayer at our graduation prayer service. Here's what I said:

Prayer service prayer for high school graduation:

Heavenly Father,

Firstly, I want to thank you for this moment and to thank you for me being able to share my life with each of these wonderful people. I pray that when we reflect on these four years may we reflect on all the times we've had but may the happy times be what we hold most deep in our hearts. As we sit here today, may we acknowledge you for us being here and realize our blessings for the past, present and future. As I say one of our final good-byes today may they mean the same as see you later. God, finally let us realize that truly the best is yet to come and let us not forget we have come a mighty long way! Finally, I want to pray for students everywhere. God, let our graduation rate increase and please equip our young people with the skills to run this world tomorrow.

This asked in your name,

Amen

I knew that I'd treat people the way I wanted to be treated, and for many years I overcompensated in relationships not understanding that I was giving of myself in order to be given back in the same way. Yet people weren't me. They didn't have my experiences and I had to understand that many had no ill intentions. Sometimes I was merely doing too much ...hoping someone would mirror my effort and I'd be number one in someone's life.

I'd be lying if I didn't say that I still haven't had that place in someone's life. I do not know why it is so important to be number one in someone's life, but I think of how special it is to mean that much to someone. While I am grateful for the love I do have, I sometimes feel as if it's pauper love. To clarify, I think about love in terms of levels. The highest levels being parent to child and husband and wives. Since I am not married and my relationship with my birth mother is strained (my father is deceased), the closest level I have even with the strongest love is probably level 2. I feel like most of the love I receive is pauper love because it's not the richest form of love in people's lives so it shows up differently. I've learned over the years that if I express that I want to be loved differently or the way I see them love others I am usually met with shock.

How dare I have these expectations? I am not their child or their wife so I must remain in my place and appreciate the love that I receive. This is extremely hard for me and brings me to tears as I write this but this is my reality and it hurts no less throughout the years. What makes it harder is that when I love there aren't those degrees of separation so I end up loving people much more than they love me which leaves me hurt in the end. What's even sadder is that I am the only one hurt by this as their love for me isn't on that level so that deep level of hurt belongs to me. No worries. Therapy keeps me grounded and helps me to accept things for what they are.

As I wrap up this chapter, I must discuss my senior quote... It read, "Somewhere down this road... I know someone's waiting. Years of dreams just can't be wrong...arms will open wide, I'll be safe and wanted...finally home where I belong."

Those are the lyrics to a song sung by the late Aaliyah in the movie Anastasia, which is about a girl who discovers she's royalty and she's on a quest to get back to her original family.

When that song was popular, there was a channel on TV called "The Box," . "The Box was a channel that ended in the early 2000's . It was a channel where you'd call a number and request any music video you wanted played on TV live. Yet they'd charge the phone company a fee each time. I called several times in a row to hear that song and I remember my foster mom got that bill and boy did I lie about that one! That was one of the only times I lied myself out of trouble! But that song gave me hope. Arms will open wide...I'll be safe and wanted. It won't be a regular hug but the ones you give out when the love touches you deep in your soul. The type of love where you know they'd protect you so for once you could relax because they had your back.

Ch.11

MISSION TO FINISH COLLEGE

One of my college letters (This is a rough draft with minimum editing to preserve authenticity)

I have had a very hard life, but it has taught me to take and appreciate every opportunity that comes toward me. I am constantly reminded of the outcome of my life if I do not strive to do my best. Everytime I take a step forward, that feeling keeps me going. I know if I want to get where I want to be in life, where I need to be in life, it starts with college.

I have had many setbacks. I have encountered many who wanted nothing more than to see me fail and wear my plaque of adversity as an excuse. I have refused to accept that. I am thankful that God is what he is to me. He has reminded me that the devil sends negative thoughts in human form to disguise his rooting for me to fail. God in turn has given me the power to lift the veil of deceit and accept nothing less than I am capable of having.

I have lived in a lot of different environments. Growing up as a foster child, my life was based on survival. The only thing on my mind on a day-to-day basis was how I could survive, and what I needed to do. That is when the Lord blessed me. He sent angels in human form to remind me of his love and the miraculous, outstanding talents I have to offer the world. When people decided to treat me as if I were not much and decided not to give me much, it taught me that I wanted to share and give as much as I have. It taught me to see and feel just how wonderful it truly is to give and receive.

I moved into and out of foster homes from the age of 4 until the age of 7. In these foster homes, I endured the greatest of abuse and grew up being confused. However, I possessed the will to carry on through it all. Regardless of what was going on outside of school, I was eager to learn.

At the age of 7, nurturing became a big part of my life. I was in a home where I was in a book club and encouraged to succeed. I was somewhat a normal child and it showed in me. I no longer hid in corners or acted in any way mysterious. My mind flourished and I always kept high marks.

This drive lasted until high school. I graduated from middle school at the top of my class and arrived at Messmer High with a four-year scholarship. At home, my marks were not so high and I was beginning to suffer from a lot of mental anguish and abuse. My grades went from above average to average. By sophomore year, I had collected average grades, knowing full well that they were far below my potential. Yet, outside of school, I moved three times during my sophomore year and twice as a junior. I had to learn new rules, new environments and new people, and my grades reflected it.Through it all, I knew I would succeed. The drive was always there, just momentarily postponed. I know I will succeed. It is just when my life was not steady, neither were my grades. But when I learned to separate the two and use the negative things to make the positive things stronger, I am where I stand now. I am very dynamic, a noted leader and dedicated to all in which I believe. I am strong and committed which I know will get me where I need to be.

I have very strong character. I am a very compassionate person and I want to help as much as I can. I like to be involved in positive things that make a difference. I am constantly giving advice to children and even without me encouraging, they always seem to flock to me. I once had a problem where children at The Mary Ryan Boys and Girls Club would follow me around, and I was referred to as childish. An adult that knew me stated to these people, who knew not what they saw, that I was not to blame. If kids wanted to follow me around, that was an attribute rather than something that should make me feel bad.

My goal is to succeed at all I try. I want to someday own a fine arts studio and have some type of housing for foster children. This place will be different from a shelter or group home. In this place, children will realize their beauty and their worth and know where they can go in life. They are not going to have what is left over, nor will they be in need. They will learn how to give back and will get many things, but first they will get love and in turn learn how to love themselves. I want to get a degree in education. That will be the stepping stone for me to get to where I need to be. To achieve these goals, I am going to be very active in college as well as my community. All my life, I've wanted to be an activist for change. Outside of studying education, writing and fine arts, I want to be a mentor. One day, I want to write an autobiography and become a motivational speaker. I also want to be a foster mother and probably adopt children.

After college, I want to settle down and find me a good husband to help me raise our children. Together we will instill morals, leadership and the importance of an education. Separately, I will be either a lawyer or teacher and doing the motivational speaking and writing on the side. Secretly, I have dreams of becoming a singer and an actress while having a charity that personally reaches out to children and the less fortunate alike.

In 5 years, I hope to be either teaching or teaching and going to law school. I will be investing my time in some community projects and I will probably have a foster child by that time. I will be beginning to pay for my house and marveling at what I have become. Finally, if it is God's will, I will be a singer or an actress.

Sometimes I feel setbacks in my life, but I know that God has a plan for me. As long as I follow and obey his commands, I am where I need to be. Some people think my dreams are too far-fetched. I truly believe with God all things are possible. I know I came from where hope was scarce and I know my possibilities. I also know that I can truly go wherever I want to.

Letter I sent my freshman year to Mrs. Evans (9/28/2004)

i thought you would be there for me. the struggle is even harder b/c i feel there is no one here fighting for me. you know charisma and i don't talk that much and i am still observing the girls here. i am not asking for you to participate in any of the events here, just sometimes show you care. imagine yourself in my shoes. just got

out of system, parents don't give a damn, embarking on a new journey that is already scary. I can laugh and smile every day but my insides say something else. i do not want you to confuse the gratitude i have w/ this message I am sending you, i just want you to place yourself back at Whitewater and everything is new and no one calls you. No one even in the smallest sense act like they care. what would you want? just think about it okay?
Dianne

Starting college for me was a whirlwind of emotions. Initially I was disappointed that I was losing my last summer of "childhood". I was a part of the EOP program and that required we spent our summer getting acclimated. That summer actually turned out to be amazing.

We lived in McCormick Dorm (which has now been destroyed in 2019). It was a round dorm with very small rooms. The cool thing was these dorms were built for two (though small) and we got our own room! We had to attend a couple classes but they had field trips weekly, free food daily, and a stipend. This experience made us a family! Marquette University is a PWI (predominantly white institution) but EOP typically caters to black and brown students (it's for first-generation college students, not necessary black and brown) so through this early experience, it helped me to get to know individuals, so even though most days I was the only black person in class, when I left class, I always saw faces I knew. Also if two of us happened to have class together, I had an instant ally and friend. I also had someone who understood me. We were all black students, being the first in our family to do it at a PWI dealing with all of the issues surrounding that.

At that time Ms. Lee and I were talking a little bit and she did my little heart glad to come and visit me one day. One summer evening, we sat in her car and just talked. She told me how proud of me she was and how she broke a lot of barriers and curses in her family. At that time she was supporting her mother and little sister and she felt glad to be able to take care of them. What I didn't tell her was that I was proud of her! Long gone was her red Sunfire (who's plate I memorized because I was obsessed with her) and here we were sitting in a drop top. She still was the epitome of kindness and beauty to me and I felt so special that she'd come out and offer me advice and encouragement.

Before I get to the dark side of Marquette University, I do want to say that overall I had an amazing experience... so much that I did it twice (obtained my Master's degree from there as well).

However, attending a PWI requires a high amount of self-esteem. Every semester started the same. For the first two weeks I was stared at for any small move I made. If I put on lip gloss, heads turned. If I ate something, heads turned, etc. Then when there were times where I had to work with partners and no one wanted to work with me. I actually enjoyed that part because secretly I did not want to work with them, either. Then, as the term progressed, I'd hear "You are so articulate" (which is a microaggression), and I had people who wanted to work with me so I could do the bulk/all of the work!

Outside of class was not much different. My freshman year, I had a triple dorm room with two white roommates. In my mind I had a plan to open my mind. Prior to Marquette, my experiences with white people were not good ones. Most intimately, it came from teachers and social workers. My experience with white teachers was OK. I either had some closeted racist (that I'd be able to reflect and see and understand later in life... I did not get it then), ones that wanted to save me to make themselves feel better or some genuine ones who truly loved the work that they did.

But because my most intimate relationships with white people were social workers or people in the social service field, I did not have very positive views of white people. I was hopeful that my experience could change.

I was the first to arrive at the dorm. Mrs. Evans brought me and helped me with my luggage (which was her graduation gift to me). I immediately began to feel out of place and it wasn't because I was at a predominantly white institution, but I felt the weight of not having a parent. I remember someone came to introduce themselves and they asked me who Mrs.Evans was to me and I just went blank. Later she decided that she'd be my godmother and that's how I could introduce her to people. We tried to find a name other than Mrs. Evans but we couldn't find one.

So here I was, the first to arrive in an all-girl dorm called Cobeen. There were three beds. Two bunked and the other was a single. I decided to get the single bed and just like that Mrs. Evans bid her adieu and she left.

Two white girls by the name of Allison and Jenna arrived not too long later. Imagine the looks on their faces when they met me. I had spoken with Jenna on the phone prior to move-in to try to get to know each other (her idea) but I used my code-switching voice. After their parents left, Jenna came up with this bright idea to reconfigure the room. By the time it was done, I was in a bunk bed and she had turned the single bed into a loft for her. She said we would switch off with the single bed. To this day, I don't know how she swindled me out of my bed.

Being roommates with white people started off OK. We were all misfits. Jenna was raised in a single-parent home with a mother who was obsessed with her being a size zero " like all her friends." She once came home and told me that her mother came to visit and they took a trip to the mall. When she found out that she gained weight and was now a size 5, she refused to buy her anything but shoes. So she decided to starve herself. That lasted half a day until she declared, "Screw that, I'm hungry."

Allison came from a two-parent home but was a freshman with a baby. She said that she was raped but that was after a conversation we had where Jenna and I professed to be virgins. Several things happened later that made me suspect that maybe she was lying about the whole rape thing.

We had discussions early on to try to make our living environment as hospitable for everyone involved. I tried my best to understand that black people and white people came from two different worlds. They liked the room cold no matter what season. I told them I couldn't do fans but they could turn the fans directly on them would be fine but leaving windows open was an absolute no. I told them I couldn't sleep in complete darkness and they agreed to allow me to keep the small light by the door on. In general, we agreed to respect each other's property and things.

I learned that black people had some unwritten rules that white people knew nothing about. One of them being that you don't converse with people while they are on the phone and are not supposed to eavesdrop. Obviously the person knows you can hear them but you are not to engage or show any signs that you are listening. Well someone should have told Jenna because she loved to engage in my conversations! I remember I was having a conversation with my friend Ashley as she was getting ready to visit. I was describing the path behind the house so that she would know when she was close. Then Jenna interrupted me saying something along the lines of "No, that path doesn't curve like that." Ashley was like, "Girl, she doesn't know not to eavesdrop in black folks' convos?" and we both burst out laughing because we knew she didn't have a clue.

Then there was a time I was studying late in the evening and Jenna was getting ready to go out with friends to a party. She saw me studying and asked if I minded if a few friends came over to hang out. I saw nothing wrong with that as hanging out meant to me maybe watching a little TV, engaging in a conversation or simply chilling. Either Jenna had a completely different definition of what hanging out meant or she knowingly deceived me to get what she wanted. These white students were nice to me but not respectful to the fact that I was studying. They were loud, played loud music, threw popcorn around the room etc. I had to stop studying altogether and decided to analyze this hanging out scenario. I was completely enthralled with the idea that white and black people could say the same thing and have two completely different understandings.

Allison and Jenna were two different types of white people. Jenna was the pop white girl. She liked pop music, wore the popular clothes and did what the culture shows white people traditionally do like go to parties and get drunk. Allison was a nerdy white girl. She told us how she dressed in cosplay and she and her friends would go into a wooded area to play dungeons and dragons with plastic swords. They were from two different worlds and so none of us really were friends but we had small conversations about our lives here and there. Jenna and I would talk about Allison behind her back and Allison and I would talk about Jenna behind hers.

Allison's parents had her baby most of the time but every day around noon they'd bring her to spend a few hours. Allison was busy trying to do school work while her son was fighting for attention. His scheduled visit was always my naptime before my evening classes. Well I spent it listening to him yell "Mama...mama..." over and over. She catered to him as she saw fit and it appeared that she wasn't the least bit worried that I was trying to nap. I never said anything to Allison about it and that's the detriment of being non-confrontational.

One thing that Jenna and I found hilarious and disturbing about Allison was that she chose to walk around nude. In her defense, she was the first to get up in the morning and we were sleeping, but we thought it only made sense to wear a towel when others were present. One thing Allison and I loved to discuss about Jenna was how much she partied and how drunk she would get.

One time I was home relaxing (late at night) and Jenna came home after a party. She brought a boy into our room and she thought that I was asleep. She and the guy exchanged a long tongue wrestle before deciding to leave. Later that night I heard her friends laughing as she was opening up doors thinking she was going back into her room. Eventually she found the correct door and she came and laid on the floor where she regurgitated all she had drank and ate right in the middle of the floor! Not too long later, some of her friends came into the room to check on her. They asked me to watch her that night to ensure she was OK. I was annoyed because she was not my friend and I felt no responsibility or obligation to her. However morally I continued to wake up and note her breathing because I couldn't sleep thinking she might be dead.

Imagine my surprise when one day I noticed a strange interaction between Allison and Jenna. Other than them talking to me randomly, they never really talked to each other. Well, I came in from a gospel choir rehearsal and saw them having an intense dialogue. The Holy Spirit and their faces exposed all they were discussing and that topic was ME! They looked so confused. They knew I had practice Wednesday nights and either I came home earlier than they expected or they were in their conversation so deeply, they lost track of time. I heard God speak clearly to me at that moment, "They are trying to create a case against you...get your facts together."

That was all I needed! I had no emotions toward them as I had already known what white people were capable of. I started compiling my list from Jenna's underage drinking to windows being open in the winter even though we agreed that we wouldn't do that to Allison ignoring her child which disturbed my rest.

Before I knew it we were in the resident advisor's office sorting differences that they could've come to me about!

Jenna and Allison alike were saying how I liked the room too hot and it caused their computers to overheat. One of them expressed that her computer couldn't turn on and it may have suffered irreparable damage! Then they went on about the door light being on even though we agreed that it was OK!

I wasn't bothered by their allegations. I was more so relieved that they didn't have anything serious that I had done and this was clearly a case of racism. Now it was my turn to speak and Kay Byrd-Egging (I'll never forget that name because whose last names coordinate like that?) told me that this was not a "blaming meeting". I asked her, "Then what do you call what they were doing?" All of these thoughts began to swirl in my head and I thought about how me defending myself in any capacity was likely to be labeled aggressive and only through God would I be able to win this 3-1 fight.

I began to calmly wait for their explanation when Jenna blurted out, "I can't do this anymore... I can't live with her," Allison echoed the same sentiments. So Kay turned to me and said, "Well two of them don't want to live with you, so it would be best that you move." All of a sudden, I felt this surge of "I don't know who you think you is" and I let all of them know, if they have the problem, then they can leave! And with that, they were gone and now I had three beds with more space than I ever had to myself and I was not perturbed one bit! Throughout life I continue to see God say to people through his interference, "Don't mess with her."

About a year later I saw some of Jenna's friends who were so excited to greet me! They asked, "Did you hear what happened to Jenna?" I said, "No" and eagerly waited for the tea. They said, "Oh, we decided to move into an apartment together (Renee Row apartments which are very expensive) and she couldn't afford the rent so she got evicted and had to move back home." I just told them that I was shocked and we went on our way. But for me, I thought about how she tried to get me kicked out and ended up with no place to go. I don't necessarily rejoice in her failure but I do breathe a sigh of relief for my vindication. Stop messing with me! Especially when I am doing everything I can to be understanding and accommodating! Oh that motif has and continues to play out in my life! God is truly a protector and that is why I try not to seek revenge because his revenge is always sweeter.

Dorm life came and went and the thing about being a former foster child is when you become an adult, most of the tools that come from healthy familial relationships don't exist. This is when Mrs. Evans would take the reins and I am eternally grateful for the role she played during this time.

It was the summer of 2005, and I had nowhere to go. Mrs. Evans informed me that it was time to get a bank account and my first apartment. She found me a studio apartment on campus and convinced the landlord to take me. He was nervous. Mrs. Evans couldn't cosign as she hadn't discussed that with her husband and had witnessed some of my financial instability and I had no credit history. She presented the check for the first month's rent and security deposit and promised that while she couldn't be a cosigner, she would guarantee that rent would get paid and he said OK and I had my first apartment that I would have the sole responsibility of paying for. Not too long after that Mrs. Evans took me to the JCPenney Outlet to get a couch that had a bed inside. Since I had a studio, it would be the perfect piece to turn my living room into a bedroom at night. My former foster mother Maria and I attended the same church at the time and talked every now and then. She provided me with a used table and used chairs as well as dishes she bought to help make sure I was set to have a place to eat and dishes to eat on as well.

I've recently found some receipts from that time period and I think about how $300 + utilities was a struggle for me. I've thought about how my children won't ever have to rent but will go from my home to their own home unless they choose otherwise. I've thought about how they will enter the world with savings from themselves and from me.

I struggled to pay my bills. There were times where I had holes in my flats in the middle of winter because I couldn't afford anything. I worked part time so I paid my bills with refund checks and part-time jobs. I remember being so envious of people with Uggs and sweater boots. I went to church faithfully on the bus during this time. I struggled to understand God sometimes because I saw teens and young adults that I grew up with who did not come to church regularly but would come to church with nice cars and shoes. Sometimes I would ask God how this was fair. I was paying tithes as consistently as I could and I felt very low.

I even applied for food stamps. They gave me a provisional approval. I received $150 for three months then my case would be up for review. When I went under review, they denied me saying that I didn't work enough hours but I could appeal the decision, so I decided to appeal. At the appeal there was a white man with a tape recorder. His job was to ask questions and he would pass the audio over to the committee who makes those decisions. I explained how I worked only part-time because I was a full-time college student and I had no parental support. He rolled his eyes and mocked my words when I talked by mouthing them! I was shocked and appalled but didn't speak as I knew I'd appear crazy because this was a tape recording and not a video. I talked to God in my head and told him how this fat, ugly, pig must receive his wrath. I was not surprised weeks later when I received my denial in the mail.

I knew my appeal would be overturned but I was more crushed by how I was treated. How could you roll your eyes at my story? How could you treat somebody like that who was trying to make something of themselves? What I learned about the system is that it isn't designed for people who are really trying to get themselves together. They wanted me to work full-time in order to get food stamps. Me being at a private, prestigious university did not matter. Adulthood and even harsher realities were hitting me. Yet even in the midst of times like these, God always sent sweet people who reminded me that God was there and not to worry about people who did not mean me well because he had a plan for my life.

The financial struggle continued. One day I had $20 to my name that I was trying to stretch to payday that Friday. By Wednesday I had $13 left but I was very hungry. This memory is vivid. It was winter and I was walking through The Union. I was getting ready to pass the food court and so I told God, "I can't do this... I'm hungry!" and I proceeded to buy myself a cheeseburger and fries. I was so satisfied at the moment but I knew that I was unsure how I'd eat the rest of the week. I took the rest of my change and proceeded to walk outside. I took a few steps before I realized that there was a $20 bill sitting in the snow! It was as if no one else could see it or my excitement! I couldn't believe God would be so good to me! The scripture is sincerely true:

(Matthew 6:26-34) "Look at the birds of the air, for they neither sow nor reap nor gather into barns; yet your heavenly Father feeds them. Are you not of more value than they? ...31 "Therefore do not worry, saying, 'What shall we eat?' or 'What shall we drink?' or 'What shall we wear?' 34 Therefore do not worry about tomorrow, for tomorrow will worry about its own things. Sufficient for the day *is* its own trouble.

There were several instances where God provided and I knew that it was not happenstance or luck but his intervening. There was another time where I had to go see a professor at his request. I was so nervous because this was a black professor and the director of Student Support Services. I was boggling my mind trying to figure out what I did. Did I not exercise decorum when I was in class around the white people? Did I forget to do an assignment? I can't remember how our conversation started as Mr. Peete's office was the coolest I had ever seen. He had a large amount of elephants, a waterfall, a microphone etc. and all of these elements were always the topic.

Yet at some point he said to me ... "You have a bill... I believe it is an electric bill and God told me to pay it... This check isn't a grant or a loan but it comes from my personal bank account." I was floored! Not only was this the most random act of kindness I had ever received but it had to come from God! The check he wrote was almost the exact amount of what I owed and I hadn't even gone to God about it. I didn't have the funds to pay but I knew I had so many missed payments before they threatened the shut off. (This was before I understood credit and was doing what I felt I had to do to survive. It took many years to repair my credit because of choices like this that I made early on.)

Even though my step into adulthood was very much survival, I did also have time for fun. One thing I did for fun was join the gospel choir at school. That's when I met who I thought was the love of my life. Seeing the guy that I thought I would marry definitely reads like a Christian romance novel. I was in gospel choir rehearsal as I always was on Wednesday nights. Yet this night was different. In walks this beautiful young man. He was about 5-foot-9, light-skinned, thin and had deep dimples. I wasn't captivated by his looks initially at all as looks never gave me pause. I was intrigued by what he began to do on those Wednesday nights. He would come in and not sing as we all did but he would simply do his homework. That drew me in and at that point I knew I wanted to get to know him more.

I was home one night and I felt bolder than I had ever felt. Before I knew it I was in his messages on Facebook telling him that he intrigued me and if he also felt inclined, we should get to know each other better. He agreed and from there we did just that.

The relationship started off as they all do...awkward. I couldn't stop smiling when he talked to me and I also couldn't keep the relationship to myself. We weren't together but we had something. Before I knew it, I was telling all my friends and I was planning our life out in my mind.

I think he liked me more romantically in the beginning yet when he found out that I wasn't going to sleep with him, he liked me in a different way.

We started off talking on the phone. This was one of the first conversations I had with a boy (see young man here) that didn't have sexual undertones. They were centered around God, school and life. We talked to each other no less than every other day and I started to fall in love.

Even when we hung out together, it was pure! We once planned a trip with friends to see this preacher, G. Craig Lewis, and all of our friends ended up canceling. I was so nervous and excited to go with him. So we went to the event and took a quick trip to the mall. In a random conversation he told me he could float. My mind began to race. I thought, "Oh my God...How am I getting home... there is no way that I am going home with a demon!" So in the mall's parking lot he volunteered to show me he could float and he created an optical illusion with his foot. I burst out laughing but more so in relief. I liked him more after that because I loved to laugh and be silly and I saw that he did too.

After all of that we drove home. I was exhausted and he noticed. When he saw me dozing off he let me know that it was OK to sleep and he played jazz music the rest of the ride back. I felt so comfortable that I woke up with my mouth open. I was embarrassed but tickled.

Through the series of our getting to know each other, he was always a gentleman! I went to watch movies at his house late at night and he never tried anything. He even walked me home after. We didn't even exchange hugs until I initiated it a year into our friendship.

So it got to a time where I began to pray about John's role in my life. At the same time, I had a budding friendship with a guy named Zeeq who was absolutely enamored with me and held nothing back. Zeeq was the closest friend that I ever had. We would talk on the phone for hours every night! Our conversations were of the deepest context. I told Zeeq about my sexual abuse, my insecurities... etc. He never judged me, he always had some good advice and made me feel like the most beautiful, most talented and special girl in the world. Zeeq was the answer to a prayer. I told God that I wanted a guy who I could have who would play a brotherly role and that he played but he also wanted to love me like a girlfriend but I couldn't see it then. I liked Zeeq but as a friend because I was in love with John and Zeeq also had a girlfriend that I respected.

Zeeq and I also connected with poetry and writing in general. We'd write each other poems or just write poems and recite them for each other. Zeeq and I had a vibe that I haven't found since! We were so in sync and it was such a fun relationship. I think I miss those times even more because I couldn't see how amazing those experiences were back then. While Zeeq knew how to knock every wall down so charismatically and carefully, I had blinders on that he couldn't remove. The truth was I only had eyes for John as I really thought that was my husband and nothing Zeeq could do was going to change that.

Zeeq also went to my school but he was different from John. Zeeq had street smarts and book smarts. John came from a two-parent home... His father was a minister and teacher. Zeeq came from a two-parent home but he grew up like me. We knew struggle, we knew what it was like to be hungry. So when we talked there were no limits. I always made sure that his girlfriend was OK with our relationship and she was. He even introduced me to her and said he would tell her qualities about me he admired. Looking back, it was kind of messed up but his girlfriend was a couple years younger than us and also came from a broken home. Zeeq was a poet and knew how to be sensitive, this is how I think he won her over.

Zeeq used to listen to my dilemmas with John and tell me, " he won't know what he's got until you're with someone else. You're so beautiful, so smart, your body is banging. Sometimes I wonder if he's gay because it's not making any sense to me."

But what I learned was that John was definitely not gay. He had a sex addiction. It would be years before I learned this fact. I prayed and prayed about the status of John and I and each time I asked God was he the one. I felt that God showed me that he was!

I begin to see things like me hanging and talking with his father and that actually manifested! I saw dreams where several times he confessed his love for me and each time the dream was pure love. No lust was involved. It was in my dreams where I was held from behind by him and felt safe and secure. What I have learned is that the spiritual realm is no joke! I never heard God tell me that John was my husband but I felt the dreams were confirmation. What I would come into the knowledge of was demons can invade your dreams. I am now sure that demons masqueraded as John and detoured me from my destiny for years.

However at that time- I wanted so badly for this to be my reality so it finally came time to ask him.

Because I have a difficult time having difficult conversations verbally, I sent an email . Here are the contents (typos left in for authenticity):

John,

I don't mean to be seem disintersted in you. I Just feel nervous when I am in your presence. You are so authentic and pure and sometimes it seems surreal to me. You have a vivacity that is breathtaking while being so subtle John . I cherish our friendship and i would never want to jepordize what we do have-----however I can't shake what I feel... I'll be honest with u... i have never been in a relationship, no one was EVER been up to par... so EVERYTHING is new to me... and it feels so good to know that we are interested in the same things---- You alone are admirable, your spirit is bright...u demand a vulnerability that I have never had yet I am willing to take the chance even if u don't feel the same...I want to know how u feel...though I am so apprehensive b/c the last thing I wanna do is make u feel uncomfortable... But i dont wanna regret and I'll deal with the outcome... and i don't want to make u rush things or feel things u didn't feel...however...

I care for u John ...and the way u feel for me is important to me...

...I've learned that whenever I decide something with an open heart, I usually make the right decision. I've learned that every day you should reach out and touch someone. People love a warm hug. I've learned that people will forget what you said, people will forget what you did, but people will never forget how you made them feel."

- Maya Angelou

...So True

And his response was:

Engineering been crazy with these midterms! How is your midterms going? Sorry for getting to you so late, but I just didn't want to respond with a two sentence email response due to my time constraints with school. You took time to write me something, and I wanted to do the same as well.

I understand surely what you are saying. And Im so appreciative for your thoughts of me and for the expression of your feelings. Nobody has ever told me anything like that before, and I admire you as well. You have truly an overcoming spirit. We all have been through some things, but you're a physical example for me and other to see of what God can do in any circumstance or situation. And you might be a little quiet at times around me, but I know it must have taken a lot out of you to write me this email of how you truly feel. Which to me doesn't really make you nervous or shy. Anyway I at times can be quiet and at times very social as well. I guess I do my fare share observing and expressing myself.

Let me express myself now in saying that I really see a friendship between us. I been trying to concentrate and feel God leading me in the direction he wants me to be. I don't feel led in the direction for the type of relationship style you feel. Im truly feeling led to be patient and continue my education after graduation. As a young man with most of my life ahead of me, I decided now to give my life to something eternal and absolute. Not to these little gods that are here today and gone tomorrow. But to God who is the same yesterday, today and forever.

I hope you are able to see the distinctions of now and where I feel God wants me to be. I must be honest with you, at times Yes, these type of questions run through my mind like a lot of people, "Is this who you want me to be with?" "Who will my wife be?", "Can I have her now?", "When?". I don't know what the future promises neither am I am in a position to make promises. Neither do I want you to wait on me to make any decisions, but only wait on God. For me, I always use to get anxious for things and want to move the hand of God by my actions rather than wait on his divine plan. My human nature craved things instantaneously and caused me to make some mistakes with my walk with Christ. I do know I want to have a stronger friendship with you. I feel like we never really have opened up personally oppose to virtually speaking with words or talking on the phone. I know time is limited for us, due to the purpose of developing our minds and fine education, but Im working on that balance I know God wants us to have.

If I have said anything in this email that overstates the truth and indicates an unreasonable explanation of how I feel, I ask for your forgiveness. If I have said anything that understates the truth and indicates me not doing the right thing, I ask for God to forgive me. I hoped this email is what you needed to know and finds you in strong faith. I also hope that circumstances and busy schedules will make it possible for us to have a stronger friendship. And Im not sure to you if this reads as a sincere letter, but my sincerity is sincere, and I care for you. The way you feel about me is important to me as well.

Warmest Regards,

John

After this response, I consulted several of my friends trying to get an understanding of what he was saying and the consensus was clear. He just wanted to be friends and wasn't entertaining anything else at the moment.

For years we played that game. "You like me now?" ... "No, not really"... "How about now?"..."Still no" is the best that I can describe it. But John was so loving and anytime I asked a favor, his response was yes. So I continued to pray and I felt that God was reassuring me that he was the one.

John was a nice guy who prided himself on giving and helping people. Sometimes I think that that is how I got the signals confused. Once I had a flat tire, He took off work to put on the spare, took it to the shop and got the new tire put on and then he asked for no payment.

He was always there when I needed him. He helped me move, we spent several New Year's Eves together hosting youth at my church. He preached at my church, picked me up when I was sick or had his sister pick me up. Anything I asked of him was never a no so I fell in love with him!

In terms of Zeeq, I made sure that I maintained a safe respectful distance ...ensuring we both understood that it was a friendship. One day, Zeeq told me that my friend's group had some imposters. At first I thought he was just talking out of his neck so I ignored him. Yet he mentioned it again in passing and I was curious. My friends' group prided ourselves on being Christian. We didn't go to the parties and anytime there was a major party, we made our own fun. Fun could be being silly or fun could be praying from 8 p.m. to 2 a.m. We truly enjoyed each other and did our best to hold each other accountable so this was kind of hard for me to believe.

Yet he had never lied to me before. He not only told me the name of the girl who also professed to be a virgin but he said he had multiple encounters with her sexually. If I wasn't sure, he gave me dates and times. The kicker was this one time we had a kickback at her house (to counter the party going on on campus) and he told me how he was there, chilling in her room while we were upstairs. He named everybody that was there and what we did that night. By this time I knew it was true and I couldn't keep this secret that Zeeq told me he never told anyone.

I wasn't mature enough at that time to understand the treasure of that secret. So I called up my best friend Sasha. I gave Sasha this knowledge under the pretense that she'd keep this to herself. After I told Sasha she said to me, "I'm sorry but I gotta confront her." While I was so sad that Sasha was going to confront her, I understood her stance. She told me how she looked up to this young lady and was struggling and failing at being celibate coupled with she looked up to this girl who was 3 years older than her who said she had her v-card. She felt personally betrayed as she sought counsel from her and even set her up with a friend who also needed spiritual guidance.

As much as I begged her not to say anything, she said that she was set on doing it. So I just asked to be there when she did.

Sasha asked her where she was after school the next day and we met up with her. Sasha was a straight shooter. "Hey, I just wanted to know why you lied about being a virgin." I stood a distance away looking at the shock in her eyes. Sasha continued, " I know the truth. So why did you lie? I'm not a virgin. We even discussed how much I struggle in that area so I couldn't care less if you were. It's the fact that you lied and you're older than us so we looked up to you."

No matter how much Sasha pushed, she never admitted it was true. I thought that was the end of it until I received a phone call from Zeeq later that night.

Zeeq got straight to the point. "You told Sasha my secret. I know it was you because you're the only one I told."

At first I tried to deny that it was true but it became clear that it was obvious it was me. Zeeq let me know that we were no longer friends because he trusted me and I betrayed him and that was the end of it. I apologized and respected his decision because I did exactly what he said I did. I was sad as he was an amazing friend but it was my fault so I couldn't feel sorry for myself.

The time would come where John would graduate. At this point I thought that he could now consider me for a relationship but that didn't happen but my prayers said that he was the one. This left me confused and empty. I was also getting very close to his sister and father, I didn't understand why it seemed that God was putting us together but John didn't want any part.

Even though the man I wanted didn't seem to want me, I couldn't escape the gaze of perverts in the church. There were these two older men who were at least in their mid-50s at the time.

There were several strange instances that happened prior to me knowing for sure that these men under the guise of deacons were perverts and I was a target.

The first JD was the one who offered me rides to church with his wife and son. He was the same one who offered to give me driver's lessons. I remember when I turned 18 and he came to get me out of the teen class to place me with the adults. I didn't know why that meant so much to him that I joined a class where the gap between me and the next youngest person was at least 15 years. Now I know that was because he needed me to be an adult to feel more justified in his doings.

The second JD was friends with the other and gave me the creeps right away. He always tried to find me in passing to say something to me, wanted to give me hugs doing the meet and greets etc.

One day as if it was planned they both showed their true colors. During this time I'd lead the meet and greet. I always started with a song that God gave me after a nap. It went:

"You could've chosen any place to worship

Anywhere to praise His name

But we're so glad you're here

And we're so happy that you came...

We're so glad you're ....so glad you're here... so glad you're here....here in Jesus' name."

After that I went around with the congregation and shook hands and gave hugs. This day one of the JDs asked me for a hug instead of a handshake. Out of respect, I obliged. As I went in to side-hug him, he took my cheek and put it on my lips. I pulled back and stared at him. His response was, "I just wanted you to feel my beard." I had no words. I walked away seeking to make sense of this in my mind.

Like clockwork, the other JD grabbed my hand and tried the same gesture! Yet I saw the cheek move coming and pulled away. He then grabbed my hand and told me my manicured nails were beautiful. I said thanks and walked away.

Service continued as usual. After church, one of the JDs must've started to feel worried that he would be outed. He apologized in case anything he did made me uncomfortable. He told me he meant no harm by any of it. I simply replied, "OK."

During this time period, I was extremely close with the first lady of the church. We were so close that she nicknamed me her "spiritual daughter". I was enamored with Sister Brenda. She could preach the house down, meant every word and did it with beauty and grace. I loved her even more for her transparency and honesty. I called her and told her about what I had been experiencing and without hesitation she said to me, "I believe you"... She went on to say from that day forward she'd come out the pulpit and monitor what was happening during meet and greet and she did just that!

Completely unrelated but at the same church was another attempt at manipulation and exploitation by a visitor of our church. We had an event where local artists could express themselves through song, dance or poetry. He was a featured guest of the evening as he was a special friend of the host.

His poetry was beautiful. He talked about how he was a practicing Muslim yet despite our differences in religion, we were one people grappling with life and its toughest questions. I performed that night as well. I did a solo that I felt really passionate about . Later that night I received an email from R. Furqwan who thought his words were like a trance. What he didn't know was that words didn't sway me.

His conversation started on messenger where he told me he enjoyed my singing and he thought I was talented. Eventually he emailed me. Here is the correspondence:

R FurQwan: It's all good. Do you like poetry?

me: i write poetry

R FurQwan: I didn't know that. Do you care to share?

me: ummm, sure i'll share a lil... something...

R FurQwan: Hold on, let me send you a lil something

R FurQwan: Would You Follow Me Anywhere?

A magic box song hugs the night, as the tiny ballerina dance her little heart out to make you smile

Its the smallest things that matter in life, for I could never bypass the sweet denouement of our stormy night cuddles

My home is with you for my fastidious heart knew no love until you massaged it, with your emotional caress

Now were stuck in a dream-like cabaret, feasting on each other as entrees and desserts wrapped in one

Let me become your every wish, because your worth is immeasurable! I could hide rubies and diamonds in your wine glass, or place a golden locket of myself around your neck, or sprinkle rose petals and daffodils in your oil-scented bubble bath, or sing to you off-key in front of strangers,

or stand on the tallest building and yell your name to the heavens, but love knows no boundaries

For a tear can only say so much, I want you to know

Princess, would you follow me anywhere?

me: When I say that I am a Christian
I don't mean I am holy or perfect
More that I have been delivered and that I am working
To be what God ordained and he proclaimed
When he called my name and he saw the change
Not for you to discourage me
And try to catch me
In a place where I
Don't want to be
When I say that I am a Christian
I say I believe more than worry
Praise more than doubt
But I am not saying
That I don't fall sometimes
Deny sometimes
What blessings are truly in front of me
That it is not for the approval of the majority
But for the one authority

I do not hope you approve of me
But that you believe me
And that you too be set free
I am not a soul reader
And I too can be a deceiver
But it is when God and I
Chat alone at night
And when he whispers
me: when he whispers "it's gon be alright"
See I may not shout
'Cause perhaps I'm not the shoutin' type
I praise him in my way
And he says I'm alright
I work to be the perfected me
Each day tested and set free
Caught up sometimes in the devils ploys
But I get back to reality
And rebuke him
And each time I am set free
So when I say I am a Christian
I do it to show what God is to me
Not to shine or look holier than thee
I tell you so together
We can be waitin' at the pearly gates
Like it is meant to be
So instead of searchin' for the deceiven' one
Let's believe that once
We all can be healed and delivered
And let us pray for that fallen one
As if they were our own
And as Jesus said
"Let he who has not sinned, cast the first stone"

R FurQwan: Tears of a Gangster

Its been ages since we've sat down and allowed our souls to meet, I guess the inner pain and the emasculation of my manhood have separated us...yet frozen us in a misunderstanding that's destroying us both... I blame myself for your hundreds of years of external rapes, mental chains, and spiritual trauma, as my tears seem empty as I stare at the metaphysical scars zigzagging across your life... My bruised heart turns the bitter pages of time to witness yesterday's betrayal, added on to today's ghetto madness... I've been a lost soldier without a war to win, leaving you deserted and alone on a western battlefield... My sisters, I use to turn up 40's and gin as I debased you in my mind as my private sex haven, I guess I was turned-on by the perverted turn-out of the street life... Oh, beautiful black woman, the day-to-day stresses of a subculture got me handcuffed to a thug persona, so I die daily seeing you struggle to a raise a bastard generation full of hatred and genocide, although my seeds helped in poisoning your sacred garden... Maybe if I was man enough, I could've made you a waterfall, stold stars from the sky for you, or planted you a heaven... I've had to strangle the nigga in me, just to write this confession, so the dark love in me could fertilize those orchids and ferns intertwining around your bruised heart... I'm tired of traveling separate roads, I'm unable to live another day and breathe another second, if I can't caress your black essence... To say, I love you and mean it, is the pure music your soul hears... Dear Goddess, since I can't turn the clock hands back or turn over life's hourglass, I can only embrace each night and day holding on to our destiny, of me and you...us! I hope you accept my deepest apology for not being there for you, for I was too broken, too intoxicated by death, and yet too preoccupied with self-hatred to care about you... I'm back though, a new black man emerging from the shedding layers of afrophobias and political rubbish... I love you dark sweetness, that black crystal shinning in the forefront of these modern dark ages... fly with me, sing with me, love with me, in our long-awaited re-unification... I'll be waiting...

R FurQwan: That was a deep poem, I like your ability to probe into the dark recesses of your own naked soul, just to pull out the essence of who you are, a lady of God... It's amazing how a woman with such a deep mind, humble soul and an outer perfected beauty could be walking around Milwaukee, knowing that she is really a radiant star with a magic voice that not only inspires but soothes... Thanks for sharing...

me: I GOT SOME DEEPER ONES, I'LL SEND EM LATER, THEY ARE JUST NOT ON DIS COMPUTER

R FurQwan: ok

me: NO PROBLEM

R FurQwan: Are you writing a book? You need to, because are a talented person

me: I AM ACTUALLY

R FurQwan: Very good. I wrote one entitled: Fragmented Pieces of the Soul (150 poems)

me: WOW, IMMA HAVE TO CHECK IT OUT!

R FurQwan: I would like to write something with you, sort of like a monologue.

me: O.K.

R FurQwan: I'm leaving for California next week to find an agent, so I'm attending a writing conference retreat. I'll bring you back some info

me: OKAY, COOL..

R FurQwan: Do you have anymore pics?

Me: NO.

R FurQwan: ok

me: WHY U ASK???

R FurQwan: Because I think you are beautiful young lady

me: OH, OKAY...THANKS

R FurQwan: Check ouy myspace.com/furqwan and blackplanet: Furqwan2006 and tell me what you think about my sites

me: OKAY

me: I DIDN'T LIKE THE MYSPACE AT ALL!!!!!!!!!!!!!!!!!!

R FurQwan: Why?

me: all those raunchy women that are ur friends----ugh!!!! That caught my eye, I really couldn't look at anything else after that!

R FurQwan: Well, wasn't Mary Magdelene considered raunchy until someone seen value in her?

me: so r u ministering to all those women??? And only God sen value in her and his knowledge was divine...

R FurQwan: Ms. Diane, no, those women just ask to be my friend due to them liking my pics and poetry, I have never met them before. I always give any woman positive encouragement regardless if she comes to me with clothes or half dressed.

me: well why are they in ur top friends list as if u know them personally and why was that funny??

R FurQwan: Because that was cute, the way you responded to what you saw. I just have them where there was room to put them, do you have a pic that I could place on there to show them the true way a lady should represent herself?

me: nah, i do have a myspace though but nah...u real funny

R FurQwan: It's all good, I feel you...

R FurQwan: Do you remember me?

me: yes.i saw u saturday.

R FurQwan: Do you have a mic on your computer?

me: no.

R FurQwan: I wanted to call you through the computer to hear your voice

me: oh, i don't have one, why u wanna hear my voice?

R FurQwan: Listen Sweety, I think you are very interesting, and I wanted to talk to you becuase I like your voice, especially if it sounds like the way you sing...

R FurQwan: Well, here is my number: (414) XXX-1914 Prince

me: I don't feel comfortable... I am young yet not naieve and Imma have to not talk to u aNYMORE, DON'T FEEL OFFENDED...ITS JUST MY INTIUTION U KNOW WHO U REALLY ARE...

R FurQwan: ok

After cutting off the conversation completely, I went to Tisha, the mistress of ceremony, to let her know what was going on with her special guest. To my dismay she informed me that she was aware of the entire exchange, that he was her boyfriend and she OKed it. She said that night, her 16-year-old daughter's boyfriend and her boyfriend (who all lived together) had a conversation with them asking about me and discussed how pretty I was. They both told the other that they couldn't "pull me" and that is when the contest began. R.F. was to try to get at me first and then the younger boy (who was 20) was going to try his shot at me next. She went on to tell me that there was nothing more to discuss as we are all grown and I told him where I stood.

As I reflected on these three men and why they tried it with me, I am uncertain. I did think about all the young ladies who are easily manipulated in that way, who fall into the trap of lust for whatever reason. On the other hand, I am eternally grateful for Sister Brenda as that situation would have resulted in church hurt but didn't because she stood for me and honored God.

Ch.12

ᴍOVING ᴛFORWARD

It took me 5 1/2 years to graduate college. Honestly, I prolonged it a semester as I didn't want to graduate in the winter (student teaching made it so we would automatically start at 4.5 years), but I picked up a minor which added on another semester.

I graduated in December 2009. This time, Mrs. Evans wanted to make sure I had a celebration. My friend Whitney let us use the party room at her apartment complex, and Mrs. Evans paid for catering and asked me what I wanted on my cake.

Everyone was invited to my graduation, but I wanted to make sure my family was able to celebrate with me. Both my parents, my foster mom and both my sisters attended my graduation ceremony. Though many friends and other people who supported me attended my ceremony, I was very selective with who came to my party.

I only invited my closest friends so that any family member who wanted to come could. After all the preparation, all the friends I invited came, and my little sister also attended. I had a fun time because it was great to see people gathered in support of me, but so much food was wasted because I made space for my family that swore they wanted togetherness.

Next, I started the job search that I thought would be a breeze because I had a degree and there were many districts and hundreds of schools to choose from. Yet December and January came and went, and I hadn't secured employment. I was terrified because my funds were low and there were no more grants or student loans I could apply for to get me out this ditch!

I called up Ms. King one day completely let down and said, "Y'all said if we get a degree, we'd be alright. But I'm not, and I'm about to go broke." As she always did, she first calmed me down from my hysterics and then reassured me that God had blessed me and seen me all the way through, and he wasn't going to stop being God at this point.

February came, I landed two interviews, and I ended up taking an offer from LadLake. I moved into a two-bedroom, two-bath apartment right on the edge of Brown Deer. My friend Zeeq and I decided that we cared about each other enough to maintain some sort of relationship.

He inquired about my job and job openings. We had one, and just like that- Zeeq and I both were teachers at Lad Lake. Zeeq picked me up and took me to work most days, and one day, I told him that I needed a car. Just like the faithful friend he was, he said "I got you.How much do you want to pay for it?" I told him I could do $1,000. A few days later, he arranged a meeting with a beautiful woman who had a 2-door 2000 Chevy Cavalier. It was white and in impeccable shape. Her dad was a mechanic, so she handed me a binder with every oil change and service the car had had with dates. Zeeq told her what I was willing to pay and she agreed. Before we parted ways, I asked her how she knew Zeeq. They just looked at each other and laughed, so I knew all that I needed to know.

Now, I was feeling very independent. I had a house and a car. But I ran into a tough situation that first summer after my first teaching gig.

Teaching typically affords you the ability to make money year-round as they divide your income into 12 months. Yet since I started work in February, my income was too small to divide. That meant that summer I had no income. My former boss, with whom I worked for work study offered me part-time employment (she probably would've given me more if I told her what was going on) which meant that I was scraping by.

To compound this hardship, I had a friend named Phaedra who was homeless and jobless. I offered her my spare room and bathroom. It was hard trying to make ends meet ...especially for another adult, yet Phaedra received foodshare so that helped a bit.

Things were going OK until my check engine light came on. Me, not realizing how cheap oil changes were nor how serious it would be, prayed to God that he'd give me time to get back to work before I went for an oil change. So I didn't get an oil change, and I ended up rubbing a hole in my muffler. Ms. King came to my rescue and let me borrow the $800 it would cost to get it fixed. I thought about how a $20 issue turned into an $800 issue because I didn't ask for help. But I was able to get my car fixed and was grateful for the lesson learned.

It was still summertime, and I was driving my car feeling pretty, liberated and free. I slowed at a yellow light only to be rear-ended. I was so confused! I pulled over as several others also did to ensure the person who hit my car also pulled over. When they saw that he pulled over, they drove off.

He came to my window yelling, "Why did you stop?...Why did you stop?" I reminded him that yellow means to slow down and asked him if he had insurance. He said, "Hold on." He went to his car, hopped in and drove off! I couldn't believe it! I tried to get his license plate number, only to realize that he didn't have one. My car lasted for about two weeks after that until it became a total loss.

At this stage in the game, I felt so let down by God. I told him that I didn't understand how I had been obedient, paid my tithes and tried to honor him with my life and look at what I was going through. My church had called a fast and I considered doing it before I decided not to.

I got the frantic call the next day that changed my life. My sister called me to say my brother LJ had been shot, and I needed to come right away. I knew in my heart he was gone. I called John to give me a ride to the hospital. He said he was out of town and sent his dad to take me.

Upon arrival, they gave me the bad news and my family turned to me asking, "Explain this to us. Why did God do this?" I was so taken aback; I didn't have the emotional capacity to answer the question. I was frustrated and confused. I hated having to carry the weight of the family when they wanted Godly direction. But John 's dad was there, and he quickly took over. He explained why and offered to pray with us. He calmed everyone down and took me home. Beyond that, he also did my brother's funeral which, to my surprise, John did not show up for or even offer his condolences.

I was hurt and salty on a few levels. I thought he was my friend and that he cared, and I thought this would have brought us together. I knew there were moments couples had to go through in order to know they were for each other, and I thought this would have been it. It wasn't.

Phaedra did her best to comfort me. I spent most of my days in isolation with the door closed. I didn't want to be talked to or anything like that. She said she felt sad that she was trying so hard to support me and I was rejecting her. The truth is that when I am sad, I am selective with where I receive comfort. I wanted John and since I couldn't have his comfort, I chose to comfort myself. My college friends attended my brother's funeral as two had previously lost their brothers, and we had all been a comfort to them as well. They also came to my house just to sit and hang...not to comfort, and I was OK with that.

The day of my brother's funeral brought several revelations. My family realized that I looked exactly like the male version of my brother, and that his eldest daughter and I looked just alike! I had never met the then-7-year-old Mari prior to that! Her mother was very sweet. She came up to me and said, "Mari has two dads, but she understands her biological dad is LJ. He always showed her love and made time for her. She definitely knew who he was," and she gave me the OK to act as an aunt to her immediately.

A few days later I took my "twin" home. I told her all about me and opened the door to my house to introduce her to my roommate Phaedra, only to find an empty room and a note. Phaedra had left me a note saying that she was grateful I was able to help her at her lowest point but she decided it was time to go. I knew it was because of how closed off I had been, and I was extremely shocked but I understood. As a peace offering she left a recipe for tacos, ground beef thawing and some fruit snacks I'd always buy.

My brother's death prompted me to establish relationships with his children that I wasn't interested in having prior. I had been burned by my sister's kids because of my need to overcompensate. I made sure they had Christmas presents, Valentine's Day gifts, etc. and they grew up to be ungrateful and unappreciative. To this day I only get calls or texts if they want something. But seeing how life was so precious and unpredictable, I thought it was important to give them an opportunity to be in my life and I in theirs. I have not regretted that decision.

I also wanted to ensure that I was making the right decision as it related to my parents so I decided to intentionally partake in events with my mother and family. I quickly learned that my distance was completely warranted.

Very soon after my brother passed, I went to a get-together at one of my older brother's house. At the time, he was dating the mother of his two oldest boys, who were very young. They engaged in a verbal squabble that day, and I witnessed my mother coach my brother how to be belligerent to the mother of his children. "Call her a fat bitch," she exclaimed as he did what he was told. Seeing this event opened my eyes to the depths of trauma. My brother was almost 30 but became a 3-year-old toward our mother. I saw a little boy who wanted so desperately to be loved and accepted that he was willing to do anything to see her smile. I felt so much sadness for all involved. My nephews were hiding in the cabinets, my brother's girlfriend was crying and defensive, and both my mother's and brother's trauma was showing. However this reassured me that I wanted to love from a distance. At least I thought I was convinced.

The following summer, I was talking to my eldest sister and we decided that for the 4th of July that year, we'd do a family barbecue. I had just graduated college and was making a little bit of money, so I used my coins to purchase what I later found out was all the food, games, and entertainment. My sister told me that I should do the BBQ at the park by our mother's house as that park was occupied on the 4th as many of the others would be.

So, a couple friends and I arrived early to set up and hang out. I set up the games and had the food on the picnic table, ready for whoever was going to prepare it. I was chatting and sitting with my friends when my mother arrived. She perused the scene and didn't say a word. I informed my friends who she was, and we continued our conversation.

What I didn't know is that my mother felt slighted by this exchange as she was expecting me to introduce her to my friends. So she got extremely belligerent and began yelling, "Fuck you and those bitches" ... "How are you not going to introduce me to your friends?" ..."They all hoes anyway." I looked at my friends, mortified, but remained calm and told them that this was our cue to go. I told them this was why I wanted them to come, but that we'd be leaving.

One of my friends hopped in her car, and I waited for John to pick up his sister and I. They dropped me off at home where I had time to reflect on what happened. Not too long after, my older brother, Garland, called to let me know that he heard about the exchange, that he was there, and that the BBQ was going well. He told me he'd send me a plate.

Not only did I not receive a plate that day, I heard fun was had by all! They took all my equipment and food and left me nothing. Nothing was returned and no one called to check up on me. This was the sure sign that I knew I deserved to be separate from my biological family.

That year, I bought my mother a Mother's Day and birthday gift, and while she was appreciative, she couldn't see that I wanted nothing more than civility. I believe that my mother thinks that I think I am better than them, so anything I do reiterates that idea.

Since I don't come around or call, that is the assumption. Yet if I died today, they'd have to acquire that knowledge from someone else. They haven't seen me depressed, lonely, or otherwise. There is so much to be said about the successful child that sometimes people forget that you bleed, you cry and you suffer!

The difference is that the marathon isn't televised and nothing can stop you! It is my hope that eventually we all are healed and whole and we can live in the fullness of joy that God is seeking to give us! I am still on a journey to acquire all God has promised me.

It's funny how life bites back
Lies yes they fly but truth fights back
People tried to destroy me with their lying lips
and I smiled with mine
And many ate the poison of deception
And I ate just fine
So now I'm full and there is emptiness around
Because the land was barren where u laid your
ground
I wanted support from an unstable fortress
A picture so pretty but it was all a portrait
Like Walt Disney the fantasy spoils
And many are trapped in the deceptive coils...

Ch.13

Closing Reflections and Call to Action

I wrote this book because I knew that my testimony wasn't just for me. This book was something I felt led to write in middle school even before half of these things happened. Then when I was in college and had two separate prophesies about this book come forth, I knew someday I'd write it. I've had a lot of false starts for over 15 years but here we are now! I also want people to know that I am living proof that God is who He says He is!

I am hoping I reach people from all walks of life. To reach believers and inspire them to hold on, and unbelievers to seek a God they're unsure about. I hope to encourage foster children and foster parents, social workers, and anyone else that works with youth. I hope they realize that God is limitless and will always fight for you - even when you can't see it right away. Secondly I want them to realize that there is always hope! Thirdly I hope we take inventory of who/what we do have instead of focusing on what we don't, and allow God to work through the blessings he's given us. And let's not forget: Everything about our existence operates in balance. Adam /Eve ... ying/yang...so when doing everything ...balance logic and emotion. The story of Adam and Eve is deeper than a story about the population of the Earth. It is a demonstration of self. Eve represents ego and Adam represents logic. God didn't want Eve by herself because when we leave emotion to rationalize , it cannot and we act on emotion. Logic was given dominion! Emotion is good when paired with logic because we are human beings with feelings ... but emotion by itself leads us to destruction of self and others. I've made the dumbest decisions when I relied on emotion.

"The heart is deceitful above all things, and it is exceedingly corrupt: who can know it?" -Jeremiah 17:9 ASV

Buy my journal that I created to archive the life of the foster child and provide a reference when advocating for support and resources. Pay attention to everything and get the children therapy immediately. Make sure the therapist is tailored to your child's needs. They need someone to specialize in trauma and possibly sexual or physical abuse. Finally, continue to believe in them even if it all seems hopeless. Buy my journal that I created for foster youth as a way to help navigate their feelings. Believe in yourself and the power of your dreams. Also - everything you have been through is leading you to a higher purpose. You are special and purposed. You matter. I want them to remember that God was there through it all. I couldn't create this amazing story even with my best effort. God is absolutely amazing! Support foster youth in your own way (mentorship, scholarship, awareness etc.) Believe that even when you are in your darkest hour, the sun will shine again.

Psalm 34:18 The Lord is close to the brokenhearted and saves those who are crushed in spirit... (GIVE IT TO GOD!)

I want to write more books. I have so much to say so I want to partake in speaking engagements, seminars etc for foster youth. I want my story to become a movie. I want to be a serial entrepreneur. Personally I am looking forward to marriage and all that comes with that. More than anything I am looking forward to living life on my terms. The support God gave me kept me strong. Sometimes it was a sweet support of "what do you need... I got you." or even " I need you to get this together" but in a loving way. When I knew someone cared, I felt empowered to push through. Don't forget: There's Progress in the Process and Pestilence in Patience YET if we wait on the Lord because we prophesy in parts yet we shall one day see him face to face.

Your story matters. It is a gift. It was never meant to keep you stagnant or something for you to be ashamed of. Use your adversity to remind you of how many victories you have already defeated. Life can change suddenly. Stay the course. It gets better , I promise! Your hurt is supposed to heal. Everything in the natural is a manifestation of the spiritual. When your sore heals, it first scabs and then it has the transformative power to become skin again. Sometimes there are manifestations of what was the sore (mark) and sometimes you cannot tell at all. If you keep walking around with an open wound you leave yourself open to all kinds of diseases -thus to be hurt again and worse. Let us learn from all the manifestations of God around us. God told me to look at how the Earth always is moving... so should we--- stop moving- you're dead... So seek healing so you're able to keeping moving - SHALOM

TALK TO GOD! TELL HIM YOUR DESIRES AND FEARS. There were conversations and desires I had as a teen that are now manifesting! Like one after the next but it took me talking to God, remaining faithful and "letting patience have it's perfect work." Being the 1st is glorious in the end yet, not nearly as admirable as arriving there. People often want to take pride in the leader, yet there are not many willing to lie in the trenches. However I will still be the one God called me to be realizing that all my awards etc. mean nothing if people cannot see that it has EVERYTHING to do with God and NOTHING to do with me. So I press on toward the mark of the high calling and I demand that you do the same!

Today I decided...to look at God's promises over my current situation and I got excited! I encourage you to do the same... IT... GETS... BETTER!

Finally- A poem I wrote at the tender age of 16 that I hope inspires you. (Written 11/3/20)

I Wish

I wish I could wash away the anger in the pages
of my diary
I wish madness and sadness would fire me
I wish bliss would inspire me
To rise above and be the higher me
I wish enemies would get tired of me
And they would stop trying to make a liar of me
I hope hope had a desire for me
To put back the fire in me
And wisdom would make a buyer of me
I wish that hate would make a fighter of me
Put back the strong lighter in me
Put the maturity tighter on me
Sometimes wishes come true
And I hope these do
To put a little hope
In the day for me & you .

DISCUSSION QUESTIONS

1. What moment from the memoir stands out the most in your mind? Why?
2. What insight did you gain from reading the memoir?
3. If you could say anything to one person in the book, to whom would you speak? What would you say?
4. What part of the memoir is quotable?
5. Has this memoir made you look at foster care in a different way? Social services or education?
6. What was the most important point the author made in the book?
7. Who would you recommend read this memoir? Why?
8. How did this memoir make you reflect on your life?
9. Was there a story that confused or surprised you? If so, which one?
10. Did this book make you curious about anything? Did you do any Google searches? If so, what, and what did you learn?
11. Did the quality of writing match the story?
12. What part of the memoir made you smile or laugh?
13. How did this book compare to other memoirs you've read?
14. Are there any people in the book whose perspective you wanted? If so, who?
15. What did you learn from hearing this story?
16. What made you want to read the book?
17. What did you dislike about the book?

18. How does the author convey her story? (i.e. comedy, self-pity, etc.)
19. If you were to create a soundtrack to the memoir, what songs would you include? Why?
20. What feelings did you experience while reading this book?
21. What is one question you'd like to ask the author?
22. Did this memoir make you feel like you were watching the story as you read?

ABOUT THE AUTHOR:

Dianne Jackson was born in Milwaukee, WI but currently resides in Prince George's County, Maryland. She is a poet, motivational speaker, entrepreneur, and teacher. While this is the first book she authored by herself, she co-authored the best-selling book: We All Grieve Differently in 2021. This book is the catalyst for many books she will write and publish with a goal that people find them liberating, insightful, and interesting. When not wearing a professional hat, Dianne enjoys long walks in the park, spending time with God, and taking herself on dates.

This work is special to me as I reflect on this biography I wrote about myself 16 years ago:

My name is Dianne Jackson and I am 20 years old. I discovered my niche for poetry when I was in the fourth grade with my poem "proud beauty". I have lived in the foster system and those experiences and life in general gives me so much to write about. Now I attend a very prestigious university-Marquette University majoring in Secondary Education and English. I want to compose my autobiography as well as several works of poetry. My topics range from politics, faith, philosophy, my life, triumphs etc.

This is a dream deferred! This was a longtime coming and because I am a child of purpose, I will do all that God has purposed me to do!

For more information about Dianne, visit www. diannerjackson.com

"For I am mindful of the plans I have for you," says the Lord, "plans for your good and not for evil, to give you a future and a hope."

"You call upon me and come and pray to me, and I heed you. You seek Me and find Me: Now you seek Me with all your heart and I am at hand for you, says the Lord..."
- Jeremiah 29:11-14a; Matthew 7:7

ABOUT THE PUBLISHING SUPPORT SERVICES:

Motivational M.D. Publishing is a family owned publishing company that assists aspiring authors publish books that heal, uplift, and inspire. It was founded by Dr. Jasmine Zapata who is an award winning author, public health physician, empowerment speaker, mother, and wife. You can connect with Motivational M.D. Publishing team here: www.motivationalmdpublishing.com

Made in the USA
Middletown, DE
21 May 2022

65994144R00129